Anton Chekhov: The Cherry Orchard
A new version by David Lan

In this tragi-comedy – Chekhov's most popular play – the Gaev family face bankruptcy and the loss of their estate. Even so they refuse to sell their famous cherry orchard.

The old world is giving way to the new and the fate of the beautiful orchard becomes a symbol of the fate of all the characters in this unassailable masterpiece.

David Lan's new version of Chekhov's last play premiered at the Royal National Theatre in September 2000, in a production directed by Trevor Nunn and starring Vanessa Redgrave.

Anton Chekhov (1860–1904) first turned to writing as a medical student at Moscow University from which he graduated in 1884. Among his early works were short monologues (*The Evils of Tobacco*), one-act farces (*The Bear, The Proposal, The Wedding*) and the extremely long *Platonov* material. His first completed full-length play was *Ivanov* (1887), followed by *The Wood Demon* (1889), *The Seagull* (1896), *Uncle Vanya* (1897), *Three Sisters* (1901) and *The Cherry Orchard* (1904).

David Lan's plays include *Painting a Wall* and *Bird Child* (both 1974), *The Winter Dance* (1977), *Red Earth* (1978), *Sergeant Ola* (1979), *Flight* (1986), *Desire* (1990), *Charley Tango* – radio (1995) and *The Ends of the Earth* (1996). He published an ethnography, *Guns and Rain: Guerrillas and Spirit Mediums in Zimbabwe*, in 1985. For television he has written *The Sunday Judge* (1985), *Dark City* and *Welcome Home Comrades* (both 1990) and directed two documentaries; *Artist Unknown* (1995) and *Royal Court Diaries* (1996). He has also written English versions of plays by Sobol, Euripides, Verga and Chekhov as well as two opera libretti; *Tobias and the Angel* and *Ion*. He is now artistic director of the Young Vic.

The Cherry Orchard

a comedy in four acts

by

Anton Chekhov

a new version by
David Lan

from a literal translation by
Helen Rappaport

First published in 2000 by Methuen Publishing Ltd
215 Vauxhall Bridge Road, London SW1V 1EJ

Methuen Publishing Ltd reg. number 3543167

A CIP catalogue record for this book is available at the British Library

ISBN 0 413 75780 3

Typeset by MATS, Southend-on-Sea, Essex
Transferred to digital printing 2002

Caution

Contents

Introduction

The Orchard of Sour Cherries

The less said about *The Cherry Orchard* the better. It was Chekhov's last play. First performed in 1904, it was a huge success though Stanislavsky, who directed it, clearly couldn't quite make sense of it. It's the most influential play since *The Tempest* – and maybe the best.

Why did Chekhov call it a comedy? Not because it is supposed to make you laugh. European playwrights have always been more self-conscious about their *genres* than us. In a 'tragedy' the hero achieves self-knowledge through suffering. In a 'comedy' the heroes suffer but learn nothing. Hence *The Cherry Orchard* is a comedy.

Why yet another translation (there are about seven in print)? Simply because I've always wanted to do it and leapt at the chance the moment I was asked. I think (by which I mean I hope) that what's newly revealed in this one is the play's bitter anger. It's the harshest play I know. Chekhov bangs away at the self-destructive, self-deluding stupidity of the Gaev family. He makes brilliant use of his unsurpassed dramatic technique: the minor characters parody the major ones, and in very specific ways. For example –

> **Dunyasha** (*powders herself looking in a little mirror*)   Will you write to me from Paris? I was so in love with you, Yasha, so deeply in love! You know how highly-strung I am, Yasha!

– from Act Four is a parody of this extract from Act One:

> **Varya**   Mother, two telegrams came for you. (*She chooses a key and, with a jingling noise, unlocks an antique bookcase.*) Here.

> **Lyubov Andreyevna**   From Paris. (*She tears them up without reading them.*) I'm done with Paris . . .

During the party in Act Three, Charlotta ventriloquises and thereby makes ridiculous the romantic conversation she has

overheard between Anya and Trofimov. And then at the end
of the play –

Gaev   Charlotta's happy, she's singing!

Charlotta (*picks up a bundle that looks like a baby in a
swaddling cloth*) Baby, baby, bye bye, baby . . . (*the baby's cry
is heard: Wah! Wah!*) Be quiet, my darling, my little boy.
(*Wah! Wah!*) I'm so full of sorrow for you! (*She throws the
bundle back where it was.*)

– which is the cruelest mockery of the drowning of Ranevskaya's
son which, so she says, drove her away from her home and
started the chain of events which is coming to an end even as
we watch.

'You stupid people!' Chekhov seems to be waving his fists,
'You could so easily take control of your lives! You could be
happy!' Or at least happier. The only character who talks
sense is Gaev:

Gaev   Let's say you have a disease. If every person you
meet suggests a different cure, that means there isn't one.

But everyone thinks he's a fool and tells him to shut up. And
he is a fool because he does.

Fools and rogues . . . and Lopakhin, perhaps the most
complex character in the play – why doesn't he buy the
orchard and give it to Lyubov if he really loves her? Too much
sense I suppose, but he'll live and die as lonely and unhappy as
the rest.

Working again with Helen Rappaport, as I did when 'trans-
lating' Uncle Vanya for a Young Vic/RSC co-production, I
have tried as before to do no more than deliver the impossible:
'what Chekhov really wrote'. Helen's delight in the most
subtle details of the text was an inspiration.

One tip of Helen's I ought to pass on, as it's often missed, is
that Trofimov is not at all an 'eternal student' even though
that's what everyone calls him.

Lyubov Andreyevna   You were a boy, a fine young
student . . . your hair's falling out, you need glasses.
You're not still a student, surely? [Act One]

Lopakhin   He'll soon be fifty, this young man, and he's still haunting the university. [Act Two]

Lyubov is sentimental whereas Lopakhin is being deliberately rude to Trofimov here because he's jealous of his, apparent, success with women. In 1904 it would have been obvious to the audience that the reason that Trofimov hasn't taken his exams is that he keeps being expelled for his leftwing views. But in fact his views are, by 1904, embarrasingly out of date. He's not really a radical at all. He's like a hippy intoning 'peace and love' in the 1990s. Yes, every word he says is true but no longer entirely to the point. Also obvious to the play's original audience is the fact that the 'Traveller' in Act Two has been sent into internal exile because of *his* leftwing views. There are lots of provocative, possibly helpful, leftwing views about but no one's listening.

And then, in case you imagine there's anything sweet about the play at all, the title. The cherries in the Gaev orchard are not in fact our common delicious summer fruit – they are what the French call *griotte*: they're Morello cherries – sour cherries.

But about *The Orchard of Sour Cherries*, as about your most embarrasing mistakes or your most intense love affairs, it's possible to say too much or too little but never the right amount. So don't talk about it, read it. Or better still see it. Plays will never be any better.

David Lan
August 2000

The Cherry Orchard

for Stephen Daldry

Characters

Lyubov Andreyevna Ranevskaya, *a landowner*
Anya, *her daughter, seventeen years old*
Varya, *her adopted daughter, twenty-four years old*
Leonid Andreyevich Gaev, *Ranevskaya's brother*
Yermolai Alekseyevich Lopakhin, *a businessman*
Pyotr Sergeyevich Trofimov, *a student*
Boris Borisovich Simeonov-Pischik, *a landowner*
Charlotta Ivanovna, *a governess*
Semyon Panteleyevich Yepikhodov, *a bookkeeper*
Dunyasha, *a housemaid*
Firs, *a servant, eighty-seven years old*
Yasha, *a young servant*
A **Traveller**
The **Station Master**
The **Post Office Clerk**
Guests, Servants, Drivers . . .

The action takes place on the Gaev estate.

Act One

A room always referred to as 'the nursery'. One of the doors leads into Anya's room. All the windows are closed.

Daybreak. The sun is about to rise.

It's May and the cherry trees are in blossom but even so it's cold. In the garden there's an early morning frost.

Dunyasha *comes on holding a candle, followed by* **Lopakhin**, *a book in his hand.*

Lopakhin The train's arrived, thank God. What's the time?

Dunyasha Almost two. (*She puts out the candle.*) It's already light.

Lopakhin So it's, what? Three hours late? More. (*He yawns and stretches.*) What an idiot I am. Such a stupid thing to do. I come all the way here so I can ride out and meet them at the station, I've missed the whole thing. Fell asleep in a chair. Irritating . . . Why didn't you wake me?

Dunyasha I thought you'd gone. (*She listens.*) That's them . . . is it?

Lopakhin (*listens*) No . . . They'll have their luggage to collect, a hundred things to do. (*Pause.*) Lyubov's been away five years. I wonder how she's changed. She always had a good heart. Approachable, no affectations. I remember when I was, I suppose, fifteen, my father – he's dead now, he had a shop right here in the village – he gave me a punch with his fist in the face. Blood poured from my nose . . . We were out there in the yard, why had we come? Some business or other; he was drunk. Lyubov, I'll never forget this: a fine young woman, thin as a reed, led me to the washstand right here in the nursery. 'Don't cry, sweetheart,' she said, 'it'll be better long before your wedding.' (*Pause.*) 'Sweetheart' . . . My father was a peasant and look at me: white waistcoat, mustard-colour shoes. The pig's moved into the parlour . . . I'm rich, oh yes, I have pots of money but cut me open, I'm a peasant through and through . . . (*He leafs through the book.*) I tried reading this, couldn't make sense of it. Which is why I fell asleep.

Pause.

Dunyasha   And the dogs haven't shut their eyes all night. They scent something's in the air.

Lopakhin   Dunyasha? What's the matter? You're . . .

Dunyasha   My hands are shaking. I'm going to faint.

Lopakhin   You're too highly strung, Dunyasha. You dress up like the lady of the house, and the way you style your hair. Don't do it. One should never forget who one is.

Yepikhodov *comes in. He's dressed as though for work in a formal jacket and well-polished boots which squeak loudly. He carries a bouquet of flowers. As he enters he drops it.*

Yepikhodov (*picking up the bouquet*)   Gardener contributed these. Said: 'Deposit same in dining room.' (*He hands them to* **Dunyasha**.)

Lopakhin   And bring me a glass of beer.

Dunyasha (*ironically*)   Right away, sir. (*She goes out.*)

Yepikhodov   This morning frost to the nth degree and the cherry trees in blossom. Our climate deserves to be chastised. (*He sighs.*) When most is required of it, it's of least utility. And moreover, if I may, not three days ago these boots were acquired and – need I point out? – squeak so loudly. What to do? Stumped. Grease them, but what with?

Lopakhin   Oh, go away, Yepikhodov. I've had enough of you.

Yepikhodov   Every single day of my life: a new disaster. Do I complain? . . . Used to it, I smile.

Dunyasha *comes on and gives* **Lopakhin** *his beer.*

Yepikhodov   Going now. (*He bumps into a chair which falls over.*) Do you see? (*Triumphantly.*) Have I made my case? My life is a – what's the expression? – phenomenon. Unbelievable. (*He goes out.*)

Dunyasha   Ought I to tell you this? Yepikhodov's asked me to marry him.

Lopakhin   Aha!

Dunyasha   I can't make up my mind . . . There's nothing wrong with him, except that when he speaks I can't understand a word. It sounds alright and he gives it so much feeling but what does it mean? I like him. He's mad about me. He has bad luck, it never goes away. To tease him the servants call him 'Just My Luck' . . .

Lopakhin (*listening*)   That's them, I'm sure of it . . .

Dunyasha   That's them! What's wrong with me? . . . Suddenly I'm freezing.

Lopakhin   They're here! Let's go and meet them. Will she even recognise me? We haven't seen each other for five years.

Dunyasha (*agitated*)   I'm going to fall on the floor . . . Oh, I'm fainting!

Two carriages are heard arriving. **Lopakhin** *and* **Dunyasha** *hurry out.*

The stage is empty.

From the next room a sound is heard. **Firs**, *who has been to meet* **Lyubov Andreyevna**, *makes his way quickly across the stage, leaning on a stick. He wears old-style livery and a top hat. He talks to himself but too quietly to be heard.*

The off-stage noise increases.

A Voice   Let's go through here.

Lyubov Andreyevna, Anya, Charlotta, *all dressed for travelling, cross the stage.* **Charlotta** *leads a small dog on a chain. With them are* **Varya** *who wears an overcoat and a scarf,* **Gaev**,

Simeonov-Pischik, Lopakhin *and* **Dunyasha** *who carries in a bundle and an umbrella. They're followed by servants carrying all sorts of parcels and other things.*

Anya   Let's go through here. Mother, you remember this room.

Lyubov Andreyevna (*joyfully, through tears*)   The nursery!

Varya   It's freezing. I can't move my fingers. (*To* **Lyubov Andreyevna**) Both your rooms, Mother, the white one and the lilac one, we've kept just as you left them.

Lyubov Andreyevna   The nursery, my favourite room, my own room . . . I slept in here when I was a little girl . . . (*She weeps.*) Look, I'm a little girl now . . . (*She kisses* **Gaev**, *then* **Varya**, *then* **Gaev** *again.*) And Varya hasn't changed one bit, she looks just like a nun. Dunyasha I knew the moment I saw her . . . (*She kisses* **Dunyasha**.)

Gaev The train was two hours late. What do you make of that? First-class service, I don't think.

Charlotta (*to* **Pischik**)   My dog will eat anything, even nuts.

Pischik (*amazed*)   Extraordinary!

Everyone goes out except **Anya** *and* **Dunyasha**.

Dunyasha   We waited and waited till we were worn out, we thought you'd never get here. (*She takes off* **Anya**'*s coat and hat.*)

Anya   We were travelling four days and four nights, I didn't sleep once . . . Look, I'm so cold I'm blue.

Dunyasha   When you went away it was Lent, there was snow on the ground, only a month's gone by and . . . (*She laughs and kisses her.*) I longed for you to come . . . I can't keep it in, I'm going to tell you my news right away.

Anya (*listlessly*)   What now?

Dunyasha   The day after Easter, Yepikhodov, well, I know he's no one important, just the man who keeps the books, but he asked me to marry him.

Anya You're not still going on about that? . . . (*She tidies her hair.*) One by one all my hairpins have fallen out . . . (*She almost staggers with exhaustion.*)

Dunyasha   I don't know what to think. He adores me, more than anyone in the world!

Anya (*looking through the doorway into her own room, tenderly*)   My room, my windows, it feels like I never went away. I'm home! In the morning I'll get out of bed, run into the garden . . . I have to sleep, I can't! The whole journey I didn't once close my eyes, I was so worried about everything.

Dunyasha   The day before yesterday guess who turned up. Petya.

Anya (*joyfully*)   Petya?

Dunyasha   He's sleeping in the barn. He says he's happy there. He doesn't want to be in the way. (*Looking at her pocket watch.*) I thought: let's wake him, but Varya said no. No reason to disturb him, Varya says.

Varya *comes on. On her belt is a bunch of keys.*

Varya   Dunyasha, coffee, quick as you can . . . Mother wants coffee.

Dunyasha   Right away. (*She goes out.*)

Varya   They're home, thank God. You're home. (*She caresses* **Anya**.) My shining star is with us again.

Anya   I can't tell you what I've had to put up with.

Varya   I can imagine!

Anya   I left at Easter, it was incredibly cold. And Charlotta chattered away and did conjuring tricks. Why did you force me to take her?

Varya   Travel all that way on your own? At seventeen?

Anya   We arrived in Paris, it was freezing there too, a blizzard. My French is appalling. Mother's flat was on the fifth floor, she'd let out rooms to local people, women, and a very old Catholic priest who had a little book, the air was thick with cigarette smoke, I couldn't stand it. And suddenly I felt so sorry for Mother, so sorry, I held her head between my hands, I hugged her, I couldn't let her go. Then she hugged me and cried and cried . . .

Varya (*through tears*)   I don't want to hear, I don't want to hear . . .

Anya   By then she'd sold the house at Nice, she had nothing left, nothing. And I had no money, how I managed to get her home I don't know, it's a miracle. And she couldn't take it in! At the railway station we sat down to eat, she ordered the most expensive dish and gave the waiter all our change. Charlotta's the same. And Yasha, of course, expects to eat what we eat, it's so awful. Oh, Mother's valet, Yasha, we brought him back with us . . .

Varya   So I see. I've got my eye on him.

Anya   But what's happened here? Have we paid the interest?

Varya   What with?

Anya   Oh my God, my God . . .

Varya   In August they'll sell the land, the house, everything . . .

Anya   My God . . .

Lopakhin *looks in through the door and bleats.*

Lopakhin   Mee-ee-ee-ee. (*He goes out.*)

Varya (*through tears*)   I'd love to give him a . . . (*She makes a fist.*)

Anya (*embracing* **Varya** *gently*)   Varya, has he proposed?

Varya *shakes her head.*

Anya   But he loves you, I know he does . . . Why can't the two of you sort it out, what's stopping you?

Varya   In my view, between us there'll never be anything. His business takes up all his time . . . what's left for me? Well, if that's how it is . . . but when I see him it hurts . . . Everyone goes on about our marriage, 'Congratulations' . . . what's it based on? Nothing, it's like we're all in a dream . . . (*Changing her tone.*) Oh, a new brooch, like a bumble-bee.

Anya (*sadly*)   Mother bought it for me. (*She goes into her room, talking happily like a child.*) In Paris I went up in a balloon!

Varya   My shining star is home! My angel is back with us!

Dunyasha *has come in with the coffee pot. She brews coffee.*

Varya (*standing near the door*)   Day after day while I'm supervising the servants I try to think what to do. If some rich man would marry you, darling, that would solve all our problems. Then I'd go and stay in a convent high up in the mountains . . . then on to Kiev . . . to Moscow, I'd make a pilgrimage to all the holy places . . . I'd walk and walk. My soul would sing.

Yasha, *carrying a rug and a travelling bag, crosses the stage. His manner is pretentious.*

Yasha   Dare I intrude?

Dunyasha   Yasha? Is it you? Going abroad has changed you completely.

Yasha   Hm . . . And you are . . . ?

Dunyasha   When you left I was so high. (*She indicates.*) Dunyasha, Kozoyedov's daughter. Don't you remember me?

Yasha   Hm . . . A little cucumber.

He looks to see who's watching, then puts his arms round her. She cries out and drops a saucer. He goes out quickly.

Varya (*in the doorway, with irritation*)   What's going on in there?

Dunyasha (*through tears*)   I broke a saucer . . .

Varya   Oh, that'll bring good luck.

Anya (*coming out of her room*)   We have to warn Mother,
Petya's here . . .

Varya   I gave orders not to wake him.

Anya (*musing*)   Six years ago my father died, a month later
Grisha, my darling brother, drowned in the river, only seven
years old. How could Mother bear it? She couldn't, she ran
away, cut herself off from . . . (*She shudders.*) I understand how
she felt, she won't believe it but I do. (*Pause.*) The only reason
we know Petya is he was Grisha's teacher, he'll bring back all
her memories . . .

Firs *comes on dressed formally: tails and a white waistcoat. He goes to
the coffee pot.*

Firs (*to himself*)   Madame will take refreshments in here. (*He
puts on white gloves.*) Is it ready? (*To* **Dunyasha**.) You! Don't
you know for coffee you need cream?

Dunyasha   Oh, my goodness! (*She hurries out.*)

Firs (*not sure what to do with the coffee pot*)   Ach! You're useless
. . . (*muttering.*) They've come all the way from Paris . . .
Sometimes the master'd ride off to Paris . . . he'd go in his
carriage . . . (*He laughs.*)

Varya   Firs, what are you saying?

Firs   Is there anything I can get you? (*Joyfully.*) Madame's
home! I've waited six years! Now if I die I won't mind, not for
a moment! (*He weeps with pleasure.*)

Lyubov Andreyevna, **Gaev** *and* **Simeonov-Pischik** *come
on.* **Simeonov-Pischik** *wears a long, tight-fitting coat of fine cloth
and loose Turkish trousers. As* **Gaev** *comes in he makes gestures with his
arms and body as though playing billiards.*

Lyubov Andreyevna   How does it go, Lyonya? Can I
remember . . . The yellow into the corner pocket! Double the
blue off the centre cushion!

Gaev A quick sharp flick and down she goes! Not long ago little brother and sister were sleeping side by side in this room, now I'm fifty-one, isn't it all so strange?

Lopakhin   Time never stands still.

Gaev   I beg your pardon?

Lopakhin   Time. It never stands still.

Gaev   Where's that sickly sweet scent coming from?

Anya   I'm going to bed. Goodnight, Mother. (*She kisses her mother.*)

Lyubov Andreyevna My darling, darling sweet . . . (*She kisses* **Anya**'*s hands.*) Are you happy to be home? I haven't quite taken it all in yet.

Anya   Goodnight, Uncle.

Gaev (*kisses her face and hands*)   God bless you. You're so, so like your mother. Lyuba, she's the image of you when you were her age.

Anya *gives her hand to* **Lopakhin** *and* **Pischik** *and goes out, closing the door behind her.*

Lyubov Andreyevna   She's absolutely shattered.

Pischik   It's a mighty long road, no doubts about that.

Varya (*to* **Lopakhin** *and* **Pischik**)   So now, both of you, it's after two, time to go.

Lyubov Andreyevna (*laughing*)   Varya, you never change. (*She hugs and kisses her.*) Let me drink my coffee, then we'll all go.

Firs *puts a cushion under her feet.*

Lyubov Andreyevna   Thank you, my friend. I've acquired a taste for coffee. I drink it all the time, whenever I feel like it. Thank you, my sweet old man. (*She kisses* **Firs**.)

Varya   I'd better make sure everything's been brought in. (*She goes out.*)

Lyubov Andreyevna   Is this really me sitting here? (*She laughs.*) I feel like leaping into the air and waving my arms about. (*She covers her face with her hands.*) No, I'm dreaming. Only God knows how I feel to be back in my own land, where I was born, I love it so deeply, all the way home in the train I couldn't look out of the carriage window, my tears flowed and flowed . . . (*Through tears.*) I must drink my coffee. Thank you, Firs, thank you, my kind old man. I'm so, so glad you're still alive.

Firs   The day before yesterday.

Gaev   His hearing's gone.

Lopakhin   In a while, before five, I have to set off for Kharkov. Irritating! I'd have liked to spend some time with you, catch up . . . You look superb, as always.

Pischik (*breathing heavily*)   Oh, she's even more gorgeous . . . Those Paris fashions . . . Myself, I'd throw caution to the wind . . .

Lopakhin   Your brother tells everyone I'm a philistine, that all I care about is money. So what? Let him say what he likes. Nothing matters except that you and I are as close as we used to be, that you look at me with those deep, compassionate eyes . . . God, God! When your father was in charge here my father was his slave, and your father's father, but you did so much for me, you more than anyone, all I care about is you, I love you as though you were my own flesh and blood . . . more than that.

Lyubov Andreyevna   I can't sit still, I just can't . . . (*She leaps up and strides about, agitatedly.*) This happiness will kill me . . . Go on, laugh at me, I'm a fool . . . Oh, my own pretty little bookcase . . . (*She kisses the bookcase.*) My very own little table . . .

Gaev   Nanny died while you were away.

Lyubov Andreyevna (*sits and drinks her coffee*)   May her soul sleep in the kingdom of heaven. They wrote to me.

Gaev   And Anastasy dropped dead. Petrushka, the one with the squint, walked out one day and took a job with the chief of police. (*He takes a box of fruit drops from his pocket and sucks one.*)

Pischik   My daughter Dashenka sends her warmest regards . . .

Lopakhin   Now I'll tell you something that'll really cheer you up. (*Looking at his watch.*) I have to go in a minute, there's no time for details . . . but I'll give you the gist. As you're well aware, the cherry orchard is to be sold to pay your debts, the auction's set for August the twenty-second, but, no, don't get upset, you'll sleep soundly tonight, there is a way out . . . Here's what I suggest. I want everyone to listen. This estate is hardly any distance from town and now we have the railway running all the way alongside, therefore if your orchard and the land beside the river were divided into plots and on each plot you built a little cottage, during the summer you could rent out the cottages. You'd have an income in the region of, oh, twenty-five thousand a year.

Gaev   Forgive me but that's poppycock!

Lyubov Andreyevna   I'm afraid I didn't take it all in.

Lopakhin   If you place advertisements now, by autumn there won't be a single cottage left, they'll all be snapped up. What this means is: Hurrah!, the estate is saved. The countryside round here's glorious, the river's deep. Of course, you'll have to sort the place out, tidy it up a little . . . all the old buildings, for instance, should be demolished, this house you won't need any longer, and you can cut down the orchard . . .

Lyubov Andreyevna   Cut it down? Forgive me but in my opinion you've missed the point. In the whole of this district there's only one feature of any distinction – our cherry orchard.

Lopakhin   Well, it's big, what else is distinctive about it? The trees only bear fruit every two years and no one wants to buy it, what's the use of that?

Gaev   Are you unaware that in the encyclopaedia there appears an essay entirely devoted to our cherry orchard?

Lopakhin (*glancing at his watch*)   If you don't make up your minds and decide what to do, on August the twenty-second not just the orchard comes up for sale but the farm, the fields, the whole estate. Face facts! My plan's the only way out, I swear to you, there is no other.

Firs   In the old days, forty, fifty years ago, the cherries were dried or marinated or pickled, and they made jam, and long before that . . .

Gaev   Shush, Firs.

Firs   Long before that, cartloads of dried cherries were sent off to Moscow and to Kharkov. Then there was money to burn! The dried cherries were soft and moist, so sweet, fragrant. . . In those days they knew how to do it . . .

Lyubov Andreyevna   Who knows now?

Firs   No one. It's all forgotten.

Pischik (*to* **Lyubov Andreyevna**)   So, tell me, how was Paris? Hm? Did you eat frogs?

Lyubov Andreyevna   I ate crocodile.

Pischik   Extraordinary!

Lopakhin   Throughout the history of this district there've been only two kinds of people: those who own the land and those who work on it. Now the lanes are thronged with people from town looking for places to rent, to spend their weekends, their holidays. Everyone's building cottages. I'm convinced that in, say, twenty years the whole environment will have been transformed, there'll be thousands of these visitors. Now all they do is sprawl in the sun and drink tea, but soon the idea will occur to them: why not do a spot of digging? They'll plant gardens on their little plots of land and where your cherry orchard was will be prosperity, happiness . . .

Gaev (*indignantly*)   This is rubbish!

Varya *and* **Yasha** *come on.*

Varya   Mother, two telegrams came for you. (*She chooses a key and, with a jingling noise, unlocks an antique bookcase.*) Here.

Lyubov Andreyevna   From Paris. (*She tears them up without reading them.*) I'm done with Paris . . .

Gaev   Lyuba, do you have any idea how old this bookcase is? Last week for some reason I pulled out the bottom drawer and I noticed some figures burned into the wood. This bookcase was made precisely a hundred years ago. What do you say to that? Surely we should celebrate its centenary. A bookcase cannot speak, it has no feelings of its own but, whatever else you may say about it, it is a bookcase.

Pischik (*amazed*)   A hundred years . . . Extraordinary!

Gaev   Yes . . . isn't it! (*Stroking the bookcase.*) Noble bookcase! For a hundred years by the simple fact of your existence you have served the highest ideals of goodness and of justice, for one hundred years your silent summons to creative labour has never weakened but resolutely has sustained – (*Through tears.*) as generations of our family have come into being and passed away – our courage, our faith in a brighter future, inspiring in us good-heartedness and compassion for our fellow men.

Pause.

Lopakhin   Exactly . . .

Lyubov Andreyevna   You never change, my darling.

Gaev (*embarrassed*)   Double the blue off the centre cushion. A quick sharp flick and down she goes!

Lopakhin (*glancing at his watch*)   Time I was off.

Yasha (*handing **Lyubov Andreyevna** some medicine*) *Madame, pardonnez moi*, your pills.

Pischik   Pills, dear heart, useless, absolutely no use at all . . . they won't hurt but they won't heal . . . hand them over . . . with your permission . . . (*He takes the tablets, pours them into his palm, blows on them and swallows them with a drink of beer.*)

Lyubov Andreyevna (*alarmed*)   You're insane!

Pischik   I've swallowed them all!

Lopakhin   How greedy, leave some for us.

Everyone laughs.

Firs   During Holy Week Leonid Andreyevich ate half a bucket of pickled gherkins . . .(*He mutters.*)

Lyubov Andreyevna   What's he saying?

Varya   He's been muttering to himself for the last three years. We've got used to it.

Yasha   The wisdom of old age.

Charlotta *crosses the stage. She is very thin and wears a tightly laced white dress. A lorgnette is attached to her waist.*

Lopakhin (*to* **Charlotta**)   Forgive me, I haven't had a chance to say hullo. (*He tries to kiss her hand.*)

Charlotta (*pulling her hand back*)   If I let you kiss my hand, next you'll want my elbow, then my shoulder . . .

Lopakhin   Not my lucky day.

Everyone laughs.

Lopakhin (*to* **Charlotta**)   Show us some tricks.

Lyubov Andreyevna   Charlotta, show us a trick! Go on!

Charlotta   Not now. I have to sleep. (*She goes out.*)

Lopakhin   In three weeks we'll meet again. (*He kisses* **Lyubov Andreyevna**'*s hand.*) Till then, goodbye. I must go. (*To* **Gaev**.) Goodbye. (*He exchanges kisses with* **Pischik**.) Goodbye. (*He gives his hand to* **Varya**, *then* **Firs**, *then* **Yasha**.) I don't want to. (*To* **Lyubov Andreyevna**.) Think about cottages. If you decide to build, send me a note, I'll get you a loan of fifty thousand like that. Think about it!

Varya (*angrily*)   If you're going, go!

Lopakhin   I'm going . . . (*He goes out.*)

Gaev   Philistine. Oh, forgive me . . . Varya's going to marry him, he's Varya's young man.

Varya   Do you have to joke about it?

Lyubov Andreyevna   Oh, Varya, no . . . it would make me so happy. He's such a fine man.

Pischik   He is a man, one must speak one's mind . . . of the very highest quality . . . my Dashenka . . . she says . . . but on the other hand . . . (*He snores then wakes up again.*) What I was saying – (*To* **Lyubov Andreyevna**.) – dear heart, you couldn't see your way to lend me a tiny sum . . . thirty or forty . . . tomorrow the interest is due on a certain loan . . .

Varya (*alarmed*)   We've got no money! We've got no money!

Lyubov Andreyevna   I honestly don't have any.

Pischik   Well, if not here elsewhere. (*He laughs.*) I never give up hope. I weep and wail: 'It's all over, I'm done for,' then out of the blue someone runs a railway line across my land and . . . gives me money. You see? Something will happen, if not today tomorrow . . . My Dashenka will win a hundred thousand . . . she's bought a ticket for the lottery.

Lyubov Andreyevna   I've finished my coffee. Now sleep.

Firs (*brushes down* **Gaev**, *scolding him*)   Again you've put on the wrong trousers. What am I to do with you?

Varya   Anya's sleeping. (*Quietly, she opens a window.*) The sun's up, it's warmer than it was. Come and see, Mother, the trees, aren't they wonderful! My God, how fresh the air is! Can you hear the starlings?

Gaev (*opens the other window*)   The orchard's white as snow. Lyuba, look, the long avenue, can you see? Stretching out like a belt on the ground. When the moon's out it sparkles. You remember, no?

Lyubov Andreyevna (*looks through a window at the orchard*) My childhood, my innocence! Sleeping in this nursery, gazing out at that garden, each day when I woke I was happy, it looked just like this, nothing's changed! (*She laughs with joy.*)

White, all white! My orchard! Autumn comes, it's awful, the sky's grey, everything's dark, and then winter! You shiver and shiver, then all at once you're alive again, bubbling with joy, God's angels have not forgotten you . . . There's a weight on my chest, on my shoulders, why won't it go? Why can't I forget the past?

Gaev   And now the orchard must be sold to pay our debts. Isn't it all so strange?

Lyubov Andreyevna   Look – there's Mother, our beautiful mother, strolling through the orchard . . . in a white dress! (*She laughs with joy.*) She's there!

Gaev   Where?

Varya   Oh, God bless you, Mother darling.

Lyubov Andreyevna   No, there's no one. I imagined it. On the right, can you see? Where the path turns towards the summer house, a little tree bent over, it looks like a woman . . .

Trofimov *comes on. He wears spectacles and the threadbare clothes of a student.*

Lyubov Andreyevna   A true miracle, our orchard! White clouds of blossom against a blue sky . . . (*She sees* **Trofimov**.)

Trofimov   All I want is to say hullo then I'll leave. (*He kisses her hand warmly.*) I was told not to come till morning. I couldn't wait . . .

Lyubov Andreyevna *looks at him in bewilderment.*

Varya (*through tears*)   It's Petya Trofimov . . .

Trofimov   Petya Trofimov, I was Grisha's teacher . . . Have I changed so much?

Lyubov Andreyevna *embraces him and weeps gently.*

Gaev (*embarrassed*)   Now, now, Lyuba . . .

Varya (*weeping*)   Petya, I said wait till tomorrow.

Lyubov Andreyevna   My Grisha . . . my child . . . Grisha . . . my little boy . . .

Varya   What can we do, Mother? It was God's will.

Trofimov (*tenderly, through tears*)   Don't, you've wept enough . . .

Lyubov Andreyevna (*weeping quietly*)   My little boy, he died, he drowned . . . Why? What was it for, my friend? (*Even quieter.*) Anya's asleep in there and I'm talking so loudly . . . making such a racket . . . Petya, what've you done? I remember you as handsome. Why've you grown old?

Trofimov   On the train a woman called out: 'Hullo, Mr Pasty-Face!'

Lyubov Andreyevna   You were a boy, a fine young student . . . your hair's falling out, you need glasses. You're not still a student, surely? (*She goes to the door.*)

Trofimov   Sometimes I think I'll die before they let me take my exams.

Lyubov Andreyevna (*kisses* **Gaev**, *then* **Varya**)   Now it really is bedtime . . . (*To* **Gaev**.) And you've grown old.

Pischik (*following her*)   Bedtime . . . Oh, my gout. Tonight I'll sleep here . . . (*To* **Lyubov Andreyevna**.) And in the morning, dear heart, perhaps you'll see your way . . . a tiny sum, two hundred and forty . . .

Gaev   He only knows one song.

Pischik   Two hundred and forty, a trifle . . . the interest on a certain loan . . .

Lyubov Andreyevna   I'm fond of you but I have no money.

Pischik   You'll get it straight back . . . two hundred, next to nothing . . .

Lyubov Andreyevna   Oh well then, Leonid will let you have it . . . (*To* **Gaev**.) Give it to him.

Gaev   Me? He can hold out his hand till it drops off.

Lyubov Andreyevna   Don't argue . . . He needs it . . . He'll pay it back.

Lyubov Andreyevna, **Trofimov**, **Simeonov-Pishchik** *and* **Firs** *go out.*

Gaev My sister's always thrown money away and she always will. (*To* **Yasha**.) Stand over there, old chap, you stink of chicken.

Yasha (*smirking*) And you don't change at all either.

Gaev Pardon me? (*To* **Varya**.) What did he say?

Varya (*to* **Yasha**) Your mother's come from the village, she's been waiting since yesterday out the back, she wants to see you . . .

Yasha Fascinating.

Varya Do you have no feelings for anybody?

Yasha What's her hurry? Does she think by tomorrow I'll have disappeared? (*He goes out.*)

Varya You'd think Mother'd learn. Leave it to her, she'll give away everything we have.

Gaev True . . . (*Pause.*) Let's say you have a disease. If every person you meet suggests a different cure, that means there isn't one. I think so hard my brain aches, I come up with a solution, then another, then one even better, which means I haven't thought of any at all. If someone left us a trunk full of money, bravo! If Anya married a millionaire, that'll do the trick! If we went to Yaroslavl and begged my aunt to bail us out – she's rolling in money . . .

Varya (*weeping*) Why doesn't God help us?

Gaev Don't howl! Rolling in money, my aunt the countess, but she loathes us. Lyuba should have married a count or a baron, she fell in love with a lawyer . . .

Anya *appears in the doorway.*

Gaev . . . and she's lived her life – what shall I say? – not by the rules. She's generous, she's warm, she has a fine spirit, I love her very dearly but, make what excuses you may, when it comes to morals she hasn't any. Watch the slightest movement she makes, you'll know what I'm talking about.

Varya (*whispering*)   Anya's there.

Gaev   Where, what, who? (*Pause.*) Very odd, something's flown into my eye . . . can't see straight. And then on Thursday, when I was taking tea in the square . . .

Anya *comes into the room.*

Varya   Anya, why aren't you in bed?

Anya   Can't sleep. Just can't.

Gaev   My precious . . . (*He kisses* **Anya**'*s face and hands.*) My little girl . . . (*Through tears.*) . . . you're not my niece, you're, you're my angel, I adore you. You do believe me . . .?

Anya   I believe you, Uncle, everyone loves you, we all admire you . . . but you mustn't talk so much. What you said about my mother, your own sister . . . why did you say those things?

Gaev   You're right . . . (*He covers his face with her hand.*) How ghastly. The Lord forgive me. And the speech I made to the bookcase . . . absurd. As soon as I close my mouth I know I've made an ass of myself.

Varya   It's true what she says. Don't talk at all, that's the best thing.

Anya   If you say nothing you'll feel so calm, Uncle, you won't get excited.

Gaev   My lips are sealed. (*He kisses* **Anya**'*s and* **Varya**'*s hands.*) My lips are sealed. There is one thing. On Thursday I was down at the government office, a crowd of old fellows was nattering away, I happened to overhear a few words, the upshot of which is that it may be possible, if I sign a firm undertaking to repay, for us to borrow just enough to get out of trouble with the bank, in the short term at least.

Varya   Why doesn't God help us?

Gaev   On Tuesday I'm due there again, I'll find out a bit more. (*To* **Varya**.) Don't howl! (*To* **Anya**.) Your mother'll have a chat with Lopakhin. He's never once said no to her about anything . . . and you, when you're quite, quite rested, can pay a visit to your aunt in Yaroslavl. So, we advance on three fronts, it's as good as done. What we owe we'll pay, I stake my life on it . . . (*He pops a fruit drop into his mouth.*) Hand on heart, I swear by anything you like, the estate will never be sold. (*Getting excited.*) Take my hand. I swear by everything I adore, if that auction takes place call me the lowest, the filthiest swine who ever walked God's earth! With my heart and my soul, I swear it!

Anya (*calm and happy again*)   What a good man you are, Uncle, how clever. (*She embraces* **Gaev**.) I'm not upset anymore! I'm happy!

Firs *comes on.*

Firs (*to* **Gaev**, *reproachfully*)   Aren't you afraid of what God will say? Bed!

Gaev   I'm coming. Go away, Firs. I can undress myself . . . Tomorrow we'll hammer out all the details but now – bed. (*He kisses* **Anya** *and* **Varya**.) In my time we did things differently . . . I've had to put up with so much. The peasants love me. Why do you think that is? Because I see into their hearts! What we believed, you see, is that when you deal with a fellow creature whoever he may be you must have a deep understanding of who he is, of what he . . .

Anya   You're doing it, Uncle.

Varya   Don't talk at all.

Gaev   I'm going . . . Off this cushion, that cushion and into the middle. Bed! Sink the white in the corner pocket . . . !

He goes out. **Firs** *shuffles out after him.*

Anya   Now I'm completely calm. Yaroslavl? I don't fancy it, I hate my aunt, but anyway I don't feel anxious any more. Thank you, Uncle. (*She sits down.*)

Varya   You must sleep. Me too. Oh, that reminds me, while you were away something nasty happened. Those rooms at

the back, in the old part of the house, we moved all the elderly
servants in there, Yefim, Polya, Yevstignei, oh, and Karp.
Well, they started letting some tramps stay over for a night or
two – I ignored it. Then I discover the servants are putting it
about that I won't allow the tramps to be fed on anything but
dried peas. Because I'm so hard-hearted, can you believe it? I
know it's Yefim who's behind it . . . Very well, I say to myself,
if that's the game I can play. I send for Yefim . . . (*She yawns.*)
In he comes . . . I go for him: 'What lies have you been
spreading about me . . .?' (*She glances at* **Anya**.) Sweetheart.
(*Pause.*) Asleep . . . (*She takes* **Anya**'*s arm.*) To bed . . . off we
go . . . (*She leads her.*) My shining star's fast asleep . . . (*They start
to go.*)

In the distance, on the far side of the orchard, a shepherd plays a reed pipe.
Trofimov *crosses the stage. Seeing* **Anya** *and* **Varya**, *he stops.*

Varya   Shh . . . She's asleep . . . off we go, my own, my very
own . . .

Anya (*softly, half asleep*)   So tired . . . can still hear the horses'
bells . . . Uncle . . . I love Uncle . . . and Mother, both of
them . . .

Varya   Come, my very, very own, come . . . (*They go into*
Anya'*s room.*)

Trofimov (*moved*)   My sunlight! My spring!

Act Two

Open fields.

There's a little, old, long abandoned chapel which leans to one side. Nearby are a well, large stones that look as though they used to be tombstones and an old bench. A path leads to the Gaev estate.

In the distance is a row of telegraph poles. Even further away, a large town is just visible on the horizon. It can only be seen clearly in fine weather.

To one side rise up the dark shapes of poplars. Here the cherry orchard begins.

Soon the sun will set.

Yepikhodov *plays mournful music on a guitar.* **Charlotta**, **Yasha** *and* **Dunyasha** *sit on the bench lost in thought.*

Charlotta *wears an old peaked cap. She has taken her rifle from her shoulder to adjust the strap.*

Charlotta (*musing*)   I have no identity papers of any kind. How old am I? Always I think of myself as young. When I was small, my father and mother put on acrobatic shows, they performed at all the fairs, excellent performances. I too performed tricks, especially the *salto mortale*, 'the leap of death'. When they died I went to live with a German woman by whom I was educated, so when I grew up I found work as a governess. But where I'm from, who I am – no idea . . . Who my parents were, could be they were never married . . . who knows? (*She takes a cucumber from her pocket and eats it.*) I know nothing. I long for someone to discuss this with but there's nobody . . . I have nobody.

Yepikhodov (*plays the guitar and sings*)

> 'And when the world knocks at my door
> I say: walk on, bother me no more . . .'

To tickle the mandolin, delightful!

Dunyasha   That's not a mandolin, it's a guitar. (*She examines her face in a small mirror and powders it.*)

Yepikhodov   To a madman in love, it's a mandolin. (*He sings.*)

> 'If you loved me
> as I love you,
> my frozen heart
> would burn anew . . .'

Yasha *joins in the singing.*

Charlotta   How they sing, these people, sickening . . . Feh! Like jackals.

Dunyasha (*to* **Yasha**)   You're so lucky to have travelled.

Yasha   I won't argue about that . . . (*He yawns then starts smoking a cigar.*)

Yepikhodov   Naturally. In far off places most things have for some time now achieved by and large the optimum.

Yasha   If you say so.

Yepikhodov   I'm educated, I read books, remarkable, one and then another, even so I can't decide: in which direction should my life wend? To stay alive or to shoot myself? In words of one syllable. For which reason I always carry on my person a pistol. Here it is . . . (*He shows his pistol.*)

Charlotta   That's it. I'm off. (*She slings her rifle over her shoulder.*) You, Yepikhodov, are highly intelligent and quite terrifying, women will fling themselves into your arms. Brr! (*She starts to go.*) These intelligent people are the biggest fools of all, so who can I talk to? . . . I'm alone, I have nobody and . . . who am I? Why am I here? Who knows? (*She goes out in her own time.*)

Yepikhodov   In words of one syllable, and keeping to the main point, what's the irreducible fact about me? That to fate I'm the enemy, like a storm that spies a tiny boat far out at sea. You reply: 'Not at all,' in which case, 'Why', I ask, 'this very morning when I awoke . . .', I give one example of many, 'did I find perched on my chest a spider of such alarming proportions as . . . ?' It was as big as that. (*Indicating with both hands.*) Another example. I'm thirsty, I pour myself some beer, in the bottle I find some creature, hideous to the nth degree, a cockroach! Or even a . . . (*Pause.*) Has anyone read . . . you know, he wrote a history of civilisation . . . (*Pause. To* **Dunyasha**.) Dunyasha, might we exchange a few . . . ?

Dunyasha   Go on, then.

Yepikhodov   I'd prefer if we . . . just us two . . . (*He sighs.*)

Dunyasha (*embarrassed*)   If we have to . . . but go and fetch my shawl, it's in the wardrobe . . . it's damp out here . . .

Yepikhodov   Certainly . . . I'll fetch it . . . Good job I have my pistol. (*He plays the guitar as he goes out.*)

Yasha   'Just My Luck.' Soft in the head, if you ask me. (*He yawns.*)

Dunyasha   But that's no reason to shoot himself. (*Pause.*) These days I'm so highly strung, I get anxious about everything. I came to work at the big house when I was very young. Can I ever go back to my old life? My hands, look, they're white, like a lady's. It's living like this that's made me sensitive, I know how things ought to be. If they're not done properly I get upset . . . So I'm on edge all the time. Yasha, if you let me down, my nerves won't stand it.

Yasha (*kisses her*)   Little cucumber! Only one thing matters: does a girl know how to behave? No? Then nothing doing.

Dunyasha   I love you so much, you've read so many books, you can talk about any subject there is . . .

Yasha (*yawns*)   True . . . Listen, this is how things seem to me: when a girl falls in love she loses all sense of decency. (*Pause.*) To smoke a cigar in the fresh air, delightful . . . (*He listens.*) It's them . . . they're coming here . . . *tout le monde* . . .

Impulsively, **Dunyasha** *kisses him.*

Yasha   Back to the house! Go that way as if you've been swimming. If they think I've been messing about with you . . . Hurry!

Dunyasha (*coughing quietly*)   I've got a splitting headache, it's your cigar . . . (*She goes out.*)

Yasha *remains, sitting beside the chapel.* **Lyubov Andreyevna**, **Gaev** *and* **Lopakhin** *come on.*

Lopakhin   Time's marching on. You must decide. It's a simple question: build cottages or not? Yes or no?

Lyubov Andreyevna   Someone's been smoking the most revolting cigar . . . (*She sits.*)

Gaev   Since they built the railway, life's so much more enjoyable. (*He sits.*) We rattled into town, had a snack . . . yellow into the middle . . . I wouldn't mind heading home now, you know, time for a game . . .

Lyubov Andreyevna   Later.

Lopakhin   Yes or no? (*Pleading.*) I must have an answer!

Gaev (*yawning*)   You said?

Lyubov Andreyevna (*looks in her purse*)   Yesterday this was bursting with money, today almost none. My poor Varya has to cut costs, she feeds us on soup, the old servants get nothing but dried peas, while I merrily scatter coins here, there . . . (*She drops her purse, scattering coins.*) Now they've got everywhere . . . (*She is annoyed.*)

Yasha   Let me, I'll find them all. (*He gathers the coins.*)

Lyubov Andreyevna   Do, Yasha, there's a dear. But what was the point of going out to lunch? . . . That shabby restaurant, awful music, tablecloths reeking of bleach . . . And why do you drink so much, Lyonya? And eat so much? And talk so much? You were spouting all sorts of nonsense. 'In my time we did things differently.' Who's interested? Do you really think waiters want to be lectured on the Decadent Poets?

Lopakhin   Well said!

Gaev (*with a dismissive gesture*)   Oh, there's nothing to be done with me, that's obvious . . . (*Irritably, to* **Yasha**.) Wherever I look, you pop into view. Why's that?

Yasha (*laughing*)   Just hearing your voice makes me chortle . . .

Gaev (*to* **Lyubov Andreyevna**)   Either he or I . . .

Lyubov Andreyevna   Yasha, off with you, you're not wanted . . .

Yasha (*hands* **Lyubov Andreyevna** *her purse*)   I'm on my way. (*Bursting with laughter.*) This very second . . . (*He goes.*)

Lopakhin   An extremely wealthy man, Deriganov, has let it be known he intends to buy your estate. The word is he'll be at the auction in person.

Lyubov Andreyevna   Where'd you hear that?

Lopakhin   Around town.

Gaev   Our aunt in Yaroslavl has promised to help. When and to what extent I'm not yet absolutely . . .

Lopakhin   How much is she likely to send? A hundred thousand? Two hundred thousand?

Lyubov Andreyevna   Oh, no . . . ten, fifteen, not more and grateful for that.

Lopakhin   Forgive me, I've never in my life met anyone so frivolous about everything, it's bizarre, do you understand nothing about how the world works? I tell you in very simple language you're going to lose your home, it makes no impression.

Lyubov Andreyevna   But what must we do? Explain to us.

Lopakhin   I explain it to you day after day. The cherry orchard and the land along the river must be leased out to build cottages, we have to start now, in fact, today – the auction's round the corner! Get it into your heads! As soon as you've made the decision – lease land, build cottages – they'll give you as much money as you like, you're saved.

Lyubov Andreyevna   Cottages, people trooping out from town to live in them – forgive me, it's not us.

Gaev   My feelings in a nutshell.

Lopakhin   I'm going to cry . . . no, scream . . . or faint. I've had enough. You'll make me do something I won't forgive myself for. (*To* **Gaev**.) You're a stupid old woman! (*He starts to go.*)

Gaev   He said?

Lyubov Andreyevna (*frightened*)   No, don't leave us, my dear, stay, please. For my sake. Very likely we'll come up with some idea or other.

Lopakhin   You don't need an idea!

Lyubov Andreyevna   Please don't go. I so prefer it when you're with us, you make me laugh, in spite of everything . . . (*Pause.*) Why do I feel as if at any moment something's going to happen . . . the house will crash down around our shoulders?

Gaev (*deep in thought*)   Double the blue off the cushion into the corner . . . a quick sharp flick and down she . . .

Lyubov Andreyevna   It's because we're such terrible sinners.

Lopakhin   What sins have you committed?

Gaev (*popping a sweet into his mouth*)   These sweets are delicious. They tell me I've sucked away my entire fortune . . . (*He laughs.*)

Lyubov Andreyevna   My sins . . . All my life I've wasted money, without thinking twice, as though I were out of my mind, and I married a man whose only talent was for getting into debt. He died, my husband, of too much champagne – the amount he drank was astonishing – and then I had the bad luck to . . . I fell in love with . . . head over heels with . . . My punishment, a blow to the head, was – right over there, in

the river – my little boy drowned, I left the country, ran far
away, I'll never, ever come home, never ever have to see again
that river . . . What was I doing? I had no idea, I shut my eyes,
I fled . . . and he came after me . . . did he even try to
understand how I felt, the brute? We landed up outside Nice,
he fell ill . . . I bought the house, for three years no rest, day
and night the patient tormented me, my soul dried up . . . It's
just a year ago I sold everything to settle his debts, went to
Paris, and there once again what little I had he took, then he
threw me aside, moved in with another woman, I tried to
poison myself . . . Ludicrous, humiliating . . . Then one day
the feeling came on me: return to Russia, to your own home,
your own daughter . . . (*She wipes away tears.*) Oh Lord, don't
punish me, forgive my sins! Don't make me suffer any more!
(*She takes a telegram from her pocket.*) This morning this came from
Paris . . . He begs me to forgive him, he pleads with me:
'Come back!' . . . (*She tears up the telegram.*) What's that music?
(*She listens.*)

Gaev   It's our famous Jewish band. You haven't forgotten
them? Four violins, a flute and a double-bass.

Lyubov Andreyevna   They're still going strong? Let's ask
them to play for us, we'll have a party, a ball.

Lopakhin (*listens*)   I can't hear anything . . . (*He sings softly.*)

> 'How do Germans earn their pay?
> By teaching Russians *parlez vous français?*'

I went to the theatre last night, the actors were so funny.

Lyubov Andreyevna   But life isn't funny. So what's the use
of going to see plays? People should think about their own
lives for a change. Most people's lives are so boring, they talk
on and on, they've got absolutely nothing worth talking about.

Lopakhin   It's true. If you want my opinion, the way we
live couldn't be more stupid . . . (*Pause.*) My father was a
peasant, an idiot more or less, not a single idea in his head, he
never bothered to teach me anything, all he knew about was
getting drunk and beating me, always with a stick. So what am

I? An idiot, the same as him. I've studied nothing, my handwriting's so bad you'd think a pig had been scribbling, I blush when people see it.

Lyubov Andreyevna   What you need, my friend, is to get married.

Lopakhin   Yes . . . It's true.

Lyubov Andreyevna   To our Varya, why not? She's a good girl.

Lopakhin   I know.

Lyubov Andreyevna   Her family were simple people, she works non-stop day in, day out and, what else matters? She's in love with you. You've been attracted to her for years, haven't you?

Lopakhin   I'm not against the idea . . . She's a good girl. (*Pause.*)

Gaev   I've been offered a position at the bank. Six thousand a year. Did I tell you?

Lyubov Andreyevna   You? You stay where you are, you don't move an inch . . ..

Firs *comes on carrying an overcoat.*

Firs (*to* **Gaev**)   Put this on, Leonid Andreyevich, you'll get damp.

Gaev (*putting on the overcoat*)   Old chap, I'm sick to death of you.

Firs   No need for that . . . This morning, you know, you went out, didn't tell me where you were off to . . . (*He inspects him.*)

Lyubov Andreyevna   How haggard you look, Firs.

Firs   Is there anything I can get you?

Lopakhin   She says you've got very old!

Firs   Well, I've been alive a long time. They'd arranged my wedding and your father hadn't yet been born . . . (*He laughs.*)

At the time the peasants were set free I'd been in charge of the whole house for years. Freedom, I couldn't be doing with it. I stayed with the master, with madame . . . (*Pause.*) I remember everyone was so happy but what they were happy about, that they weren't so sure of.

Lopakhin   You preferred it before, did you? You enjoyed being whipped?

Firs (*having misheard*)   Certainly. The peasants belonged to the masters, the masters to the peasants. These days it's all a big muddle, who knows what's going on?

Gaev   Shush, Firs. Tomorrow I'm going to town. I've been promised a meeting with General What's-his-name who may lend us a certain amount on particular terms.

Lopakhin   He won't. And even if he did, the one thing I know is, whatever interest he asks, you won't pay it.

Lyubov Andreyevna   He's imagined the whole thing. There is no general.

Trofimov, **Anya** *and* **Varya** *come on.*

Gaev   Ah, here come the rest of us.

Anya   Mother's over there.

Lyubov Andreyevna (*tenderly*)   Come, come . . . My own, my very, very own . . . (*She embraces* **Anya** *and* **Varya**.) Do you know how deeply I love you, both of you? Sit next to me, there, that's what I want.

Everyone sits.

Lopakhin (*to* **Trofimov**)   So have you taken your exams yet? He's devoting his life to the study of young ladies.

Trofimov   In what way does my life concern you?

Lopakhin   He'll soon be fifty, this young man, and he's still haunting the university.

Trofimov   You know very well, if they allowed me to take my exams, I'd have taken them years ago!

Lopakhin   What a fascinating specimen, for no reason all at once he's furious.

Trofimov   Stop pestering me!

Lopakhin (*laughs*)   Well, allow me to ask you one question. What do you think of me?

Trofimov   Of you? Well, you're rich, soon you'll be a millionaire. Now, we all know that in nature nothing exists that doesn't fulfil some function. The function of wild animals, I suppose, is to gobble up all the little ones that get in their way, so no doubt you have a function as well.

Everyone laughs.

Varya   Stick to something you know about, Petya, tell us about the planets.

Lyubov Andreyevna   No, let's pick up from where we were yesterday.

Trofimov   What were we talking about?

Gaev   The dignity of mankind.

Trofimov   We talked for hours yesterday but did we reach any conclusions? I don't think so. To say mankind has dignity suggests that we human beings possess a quality that is almost mystical. Perhaps you're right and we do. But let's reduce the question to its elements and analyse them. First, our bodies: the way we're put together is clumsy and inefficient, no one can deny that. Secondly, our minds: most of us are little better than beasts, with no culture, no sense of joy. So what we ought to do is stop congratulating ourselves on our dignity and start doing some work.

Gaev   You'll still die, no matter what arguments you come up with.

Trofimov   Who knows? What does it mean 'to die'? Perhaps human beings possess a hundred senses and when we die only the five we know about stop and the rest go on for ever.

Lyubov Andreyevna   You're so clever, Petya . . .

Lopakhin (*ironically*)   Oh, remarkably!

Trofimov   Day after day mankind advances, refining and increasing its powers. Today there are many things we still can't achieve, or even understand, tomorrow we'll do them without a moment's thought, but we must work, we must use our last ounce of strength to support all those who struggle to make sense of things. Here in Russia, among people like us, who actually works? No one! I know so many intellectuals, writers, which of them has an ambition he's struggling to achieve? No, they lounge about, the less they accomplish the happier they seem. Oh, they call themselves progressives but they treat their servants like second-class human beings and the peasants like beasts. Do they ever put in the effort really to get to grips with a subject? They start a book then throw it aside, about science they know a few bits and pieces, about art they don't understand a thing. Of course they take the world ever so seriously, their mouths are always turned down, what they adore is to philosophise – and all the time, in front of their eyes, workers eat food not fit for dogs, sleep thirty, even forty squashed into rooms infested with bedbugs, stinking, the walls streaming, you can imagine what goes on in places like that . . . so, all our high-minded discussions, what, in fact, are they for? They're to distract attention from how life is really lived. I'll give you an example: we've heard so much about the new schools for children, the libraries . . . Would someone draw me a map of where they are? You'll find them in novels, nowhere else, they don't exist! What exists is dirt, is hypocrisy and the kind of primitive barbarism the rest of the world did away with two centuries ago . . . So if I come across a serious face I run, intellectual conversation terrifies me. We'd all do better to keep our mouths shut!

Lopakhin   You know, every morning I'm up by five, I work till the sun goes down, and I deal with only one thing: money, my money, other people's money – so I've learnt something about human nature. Try to get something done in this world, you'll soon discover how few honest, decent people there are.

At night often I can't sleep, I think to myself: 'Lord, you've covered the earth with fields, you've given us such huge forests, horizons that stretch on and on . . . Living in the midst of all this, we should be giants . . .'

Lyubov Andreyevna   Giants? What good would that do? . . . In fairy tales, fine . . . anywhere else they'd just frighten people.

At the back of the stage, **Yepikhodov** *crosses, playing his guitar quietly, mournfully.*

Lyubov Andreyevna (*thoughfully*)   There's Yepikhodov . . .

Anya (*thoughtfully*)   There's Yepikhodov . . .

Gaev   *Mesdames et messieurs,* the sun has set.

Trofimov   So it has.

Gaev (*declaiming quietly*)   Oh, sublime nature, your radiance is eternal, exquisite, pitiless, you are our mother, in your bosom you mingle powers of life and death, you create, you destroy . . .

Varya (*begging*)   Uncle!

Anya   You're doing it, Uncle.

Trofimov   What you should do is double the yellow off the centre cushion.

Gaev   I'll say nothing, not a word.

They sit lost in thought. Silence. The only sound is **Firs** *muttering quietly. Suddenly, from far away, a sound rings out. It's as though there came from the sky the sound of a string breaking, then dying away mournfully.*

Lyubov Andreyevna   What was that?

Lopakhin   No idea. A cable snapping in a mine. Very far away.

Gaev   A bird, could it be? . . . possibly a heron.

Trofimov   Or an owl . . .

Lyubov Andréyevna (*shudders*)   It was horrid, I don't know why.

Firs Just before our luck ran out, the same thing happened: an owl shrieked, the samovar moaned and whistled . . .

Gaev   What does he mean 'before our luck ran out'?

Firs   Before the peasants were set free.

Lyubov Andreyevna   My friends, time to go home, night's almost here. (*To* **Anya**.) You've tears in your eyes . . . Why, my darling sweet? (*She embraces her.*)

Anya   It's nothing, mother, I'm fine.

Trofimov   Someone's coming.

A **Traveller** *comes on. He wears a battered white cap and an overcoat. He is slightly drunk.*

Traveller   Forgive me, I'm heading for the station, is this the quickest way?

Gaev   It is. Follow this path.

Traveller   Very grateful. (*Coughing*) The weather's been magnificent . . . (*Reciting*)

> 'Go to the Volga, hear the mournful cries
> That rise like a dirge up to the skies.
> Whose is the pain? 'Tis the oarsmen who haul
> The boats. How they suffer, one at all . . .'

(*To* **Varya**.) *Mademoiselle*, I'm one of those who suffer. I've been exiled from my home. Spare me some change, I haven't eaten all day . . .

Frightened, **Varya** *cries out.*

Lopakhin (*angry*)   Even beggars should know how to behave.

Lyubov Andreyevna (*taken aback*)   Wait, wait, I'll give you something . . . Come here . . . (*She looks in her purse.*) I haven't got any coins . . . doesn't matter, take this.

Traveller I'm very grateful! (*He goes out.*)

Laughter.

Varya (*frightened*) I'm not staying . . . I'm not staying . . . Mother, we can't afford to feed the servants and you give him all that.

Lyubov Andreyevna I'm a fool! What's to be done with me? The minute we're home I'll put everything I have into your hands. (*To* **Lopakhin**.) I'll need to borrow some more . . .

Lopakhin Of course.

Lyubov Andreyevna Everyone, let's go. Oh, and Varya, I forgot to tell you, we've found you a husband.

Varya (*through tears*) Mother, that's not funny.

Lopakhin 'Amelia, get thee to a nunnery . . .'

Gaev My hands are trembling, it's days since I played billiards.

Lopakhin 'Amelia, O nymph, in thy . . . something . . . be all my sins . . .' Don't remember . . .

Lyubov Andreyevna Come, it's almost dinner time.

Varya He gave me a shock. My heart's pounding.

Lopakhin Don't forget, ladies and gentlemen: on the twenty-second of August the cherry orchard comes up for sale . . . We must make a decision . . .

Everyone goes out except **Trofimov** *and* **Anya**.

Anya (*laughing*) We should run after that man who frightened Varya and thank him. At last we're alone.

Trofimov Varya – she's so terrified we'll fall in love, every time we turn around there she is. Her view of life's so banal, how could she grasp that what we feel for each other isn't love, it's much higher than that. Our goal, you and I, is to rise above the trivial illusions that block the road to freedom, to happiness. That's what gives our life meaning. Off we go, we two, marching towards the bright star shining in the distance! Nothing will stop us! Here we go! Come up to the front, my friends!

Anya (*clasping her hands with emotion*)   The way you put things, Petya, it's so exciting! (*Pause.*) Today has been like heaven.

Trofimov   Yes, hasn't the weather been wonderful.

Anya   I've become a new person and it's all because of you. I used to love the cherry orchard so much, I don't feel that any more. I loved it with all my heart, I thought our orchard was the best place on earth.

Trofimov   The whole of Russia is our orchard. The earth is infinite, magnificent, there are hundreds of thousands of best places. (*Pause.*) Anya, I want you to think about what I'm going to say. Your grandfather, your great-grandfather and his father and so on, all of them owned men and women, they bought and sold human beings. Can you see from every tree in the orchard, from every leaf, from every trunk their eyes staring at you, can you hear their voices? . . . To own a human being – is it possible to do that without corrupting your soul? I'm not only talking about those who lived long ago, I mean people living now . . . you see, what's happened is: your mother, even you yourself, your uncle are unconscious of the fact that you live but someone else pays the price. And the people in whose debt you are, would you even let them through your front door? . . . In my opinion we've wasted two hundred years, what progress have we made? None! Do we analyse the past? No, so how can we understand it? All anyone here ever does is talk in abstractions, get bored and drink vodka. And all the time it's blindingly clear: if we truly want to live good lives we have to pay our debt to the past, we must pay what we owe, then we're finished with it once and for all. The only coin in which to pay is suffering, is work – rigorous, ceaseless work. I want you to understand this, Anya.

Anya   Our house doesn't belong to us, it hasn't for years, I'll move out, I promise, I will.

Trofimov   Who has the key to the front door, do you? Throw it down the well and walk away. Set yourself free as the wind.

Anya (*carried away*)   You make everything seem so simple!

Trofimov   Anya, believe what I'm telling you! I'm not yet thirty, I'm young, I'm still a student but I've suffered! In winter I have no food, none at all, I get sick, desperate, no money, I'm forced to wander about, I sleep in such vile places, what else can I do? But every moment of the night and of the day, in my soul I can feel how the world will be, I can't put it into words. I'm already feeling the happiness of the future, Anya, I feel it so clearly . . .

Anya (*thoughtfully*)   There's the moon.

Yepikhodov *can be heard playing the same mournful song on his guitar.*

The moon rises.

Among the poplars, **Varya** *searches for* **Anya**.

Varya's voice   Anya! Where are you?

Trofimov   Yes, there's the moon. (*Pause.*) It's almost here, happiness, it's getting closer every day. Aren't those its footsteps? And if we're not around when it arrives, so what? Others will be.

Varya's voice   Anya! Where are you?

Trofimov   Can't she leave us alone! (*Angrily.*) It's so annoying!

Anya   Let's go to the river. It's lovely down there.

They go.

Varya's voice   Anya! Anya!

Act Three

A drawing room separated by an archway from a ballroom. The chandelier is ablaze. The Jewish orchestra can be heard playing in the entrance hall.

Evening.

In the ballroom the guests are dancing the grand rond.

Pischik's voice   *Promenade à une pair!*

The dancers enter the drawing room in pairs. First **Simeonov-Pischik** *and* **Charlotta**, *second* **Trofimov** *and* **Lyubov Andreyevna**, *third* **Anya** *and the* **Post Office Clerk**, *fourth* **Varya** *and the* **Station Master**, *and so on. As she dances,* **Varya** *weeps gently and wipes away tears.* **Dunyasha** *is in the final pair.*

The dancers circle the drawing room.

Pischik   *Grand rond, balancez! Les cavaliers à genoux et remerciez vos dames!*

Firs, *wearing tails, brings in a tray of selzer water.* **Pischik** *and* **Trofimov** *come into the drawing room.*

Pischik   My blood pressure's sky high, I've had two strokes, the last thing I want to do is dance but a dog, even if it doesn't bark, must wag its tail. In fact, I'm strong as a horse. My dear father, may he rest in God's peace, loved to make jokes, his favourite was that all us Simeonov-Pischiks are descended from the actual horse Caligula appointed as senator . . . (*He sits.*) The problem is: no money! A hungry dog thinks only of meat . . . (*He falls asleep, snores, wakes up at once.*) Just like I do . . . All I think about is money, money, money.

Trofimov   It's true, you're built exactly like a horse.

Pischik   So what? . . . A horse is a fine animal . . . you can sell a horse . . .

People are heard playing billiards in the next room. **Varya** *appears in the archway.*

Trofimov (*teasing* **Varya**)   'Here comes the bride! Here comes the bride!'

Varya (*angrily*)   'Hullo, Mr Pasty-Face!'

Trofimov   Yes, I'm pasty-faced and proud of it!

Varya (*bitterly*)   So you see how we are, we hire musicians but can we pay for them? (*She goes out.*)

Trofimov   All the energy you've wasted throughout your life scratching around for money, if you'd used it you could have pushed the earth right off its axis.

Pischik   Nietzsche . . . a philosopher – the greatest, the most famous man who ever lived . . . he had a brain as big as that – wrote in one of his books: 'I can think of no reason whatsoever not to forge banknotes.'

Trofimov (*astonished*)   You've read Nietzsche?

Pischik   My Dashenka told me about him . . . The hole I'm in is so deep I'd like to forge a few banknotes . . . The day after tomorrow I have to pay the sum of three hundred and ten . . . so far I've got my hands on one hundred and thirty . . . (*Feeling in his pockets, alarmed.*) It's gone! My money's gone! (*Through tears.*) Where's all my money? (*Joyfully.*) It's here, got stuck in the lining . . . Whew, did you see me sweat?

Lyubov Andreyevna *and* **Charlotta** *come on.*

Lyubov Andreyevna (*humming a* lezginka, *a Caucasian dance*) What's Leonid up to? What's keeping him in town so long? Dunyasha, offer the musicians tea . . .

Trofimov   I bet anything you like the auction's been cancelled.

Lyubov Andreyevna   What a time we pick to throw a party, to have musicians crawling round the house . . . What difference does it make? (*She sits and hums softly.*)

Charlotta (*hands* **Pischik** *a pack of cards.*)   A pack of cards, think of any card you like.

Pischik   Done.

Charlotta   Shuffle them. Good. Now give it here. *Eins, zwei, drei!* Where has your card got to? Try your inside pocket . . .

Pischik (*taking a card from his pocket*)   The eight of spades, the very one! (*Amazed.*) Extraordinary!

Charlotta (*with the pack on her palm, to* **Trofimov**)   Quick, which card's on top?

Trofimov   Which is on top? The queen of spades.

Charlotta   And so it is! (*To* **Pischik**.) Now, which card?

Pischik   The ace of hearts.

Charlotta   And so it is! (*She claps her hands and the pack disappears.*) Today has been like heaven.

As though from under the floor, a mysterious female voice answers: 'Yes, hasn't it been wonderful weather, mademoiselle.'

Charlotta   The way you put things, it's so exciting . . .

As though from under the floor: 'I'm very fond of you too, mademoiselle.'

Station Master (*applauding*)   The best ventriloquist in the world! Bravo!

Pischik (*amazed*)   Unbelievable . . . Isn't she enchanting? . . . I'm head over heels . . .

Charlotta   In love? (*Shrugging her shoulders.*) Is it possible you could feel love? *Guter Mensch, aber schlechter Musikant.*

Trofimov   An old horse like you . . .

Charlotta   Attention, please . . . One final trick. (*She takes a rug from a chair.*) This exquisite rug I'm offering for sale . . . (*She shakes it.*) Who wants to buy?

Pischik   Unbelievable!

Charlotta   *Eins, zwei, drei!*

The rug has been lowered, now she raises it. Behind it stands **Anya**. *She bows, runs to her mother, hugs her, then runs back into the ballroom. Everyone is delighted.*

Lyubov Andreyevna (*applauding*)   Bravo, bravo!

Charlotta   And once more! *Eins, zwei, drei*!

She raises the rug. Behind it stands **Varya**. *She bows.*

Pischik (*amazed*)   Unbelievable!

Charlotta   The show is over! (*She throws the rug at* **Pischik**, *bows and runs out of the ballroom.*)

Pischik   What a bad girl . . . Isn't she? Don't you agree with me? (*He goes out.*)

Lyubov Andreyevna   Still no Leonid. What he's doing I can't imagine! It was all over hours ago, surely, either the estate's sold or the auction was cancelled, so why not come home and tell us which?

Varya (*trying to calm her*)   Uncle's bought it, I know he has.

Trofimov (*sneering*)   Oh certainly, no doubt about that.

Varya   Our aunt in Yaroslavl sent him the authority to buy it in her name, she'll take over the whole debt. She did it for Anya. God will look after us, Uncle will buy it.

Lyubov Andreyevna   She sent fifteen thousand, and instructions to put the deeds in her name right away, that's how far she trusts us. Fifteen thousand won't even pay the interest. (*She covers her face with her hands.*) My fate is being decided, my whole life . . .

Trofimov (*teasing* **Varya**)   'Here comes the bride!'

Varya (*angrily*)   You'll be dead before you take your exams! They've expelled you twice already!

Lyubov Andreyevna   Varya, why fly into a rage? So he teases you. Does it matter? If you want to marry Lopakhin, what's stopping you? He's a good man, he has interesting ideas. If you'd rather not, don't – no one's putting pressure on you, darling . . .

Varya   I think about it, Mother, I won't pretend I don't. He is a good man, I am fond of him.

Lyubov Andreyevna   Then marry him. What are you waiting for, explain it to me?

Varya   Do you expect me to propose to him? For two years everyone's gone on and on about it, 'marry him, marry him', but he says nothing, except to make a joke. I understand, his priority is his business, getting rich. If we had any money at all, I'd give up everything, I'd go away, I'd enter a convent.

Trofimov   'My soul would sing.'

Varya (*of* **Trofimov**)   He simply can't stop himself, he just has to show off! (*Gently, in tears.*) You were so beautiful, Petya, now it's all gone! (*To* **Lyubov Andreyevna**, *no longer crying.*) I'm fine, Mother, as long as I have something to do, as long as I keep busy every minute of the day.

Yasha *comes on.*

Yasha (*struggling not to laugh*)   Yepikhodov's snapped a billiard cue! (*He goes out.*)

Varya   Yepikhodov's in here? Why? Who told him he can play billiards? I can't understand these people . . . (*She goes out.*)

Lyubov Andreyevna   Why do you tease her, Petya? She's miserable enough without your help.

Trofimov   She's a busybody. Not once the whole summer has she left me and Anya on our own. 'Oh, goodness, maybe we'll fall in love.' What's it to do with her? Besides which, I've given her no reason to imagine anything so banal. What unites Anya and me is much more than a love affair.

Lyubov Andreyevna   What could be more than a love affair? (*Very agitated.*) Where is Leonid? Is it sold or isn't it? We've had such bad luck, such terrible luck, my mind can't take it in, I hardly know what I'm doing . . . I want to scream . . . to do something ridiculous. Help me, Petya. Talk to me, say anything . . .

Trofimov   Whether the estate is sold or not, it makes no difference. That way of life was over long ago, you can't go back, the road's been dug up. So calm down. And, for once in your life, face the truth.

Lyubov Andreyevna   Truth? Which one? You see so clearly: 'That's truth over there, and over there that's a lie.' I feel I've gone blind, I can see nothing. All the serious questions of life, they don't frighten you, you wade in, sort them out, but, sweetheart, isn't that easy for you because you're young, because to you those 'questions', they're abstract, you've never had to wrestle with them? You gaze towards the future, head held high, because you've no idea of the horrors to come, life's still round the corner, you haven't caught sight of it yet. You're bolder than us, more honest, you think more deeply, but if you had a generous soul you'd forget all that, you'd try to understand how it is to be me. This is my home, I was born here, my mother and father lived here, my grandfather, I love this house, my being and the cherry orchard are one and the same, if it has to be sold then sell me . . . (*She hugs* **Trofimov** *and kisses him on the forehead.*) This is where my son drowned . . . (*She weeps.*) You're good, you're kind, try to understand me.

Trofimov   I feel for you with my whole heart.

Lyubov Andreyevna   Yes, but can't you find another way of saying that to me . . . ? (*She takes out a handkerchief. A telegram drops to the floor.*) Today there's a stone on my heart, you can't imagine how I feel. I find this noise intolerable, it wrenches my soul, my whole body's shaking, I can't bear all these people, but I'm afraid to be alone, of silence. Don't judge me, Petya . . . I love you as though you were my own. If Anya decides to marry you I'll be overjoyed, I swear it, but, darling, study hard, you must, and take your exams. You've lost control of your life, fate blows you this way and that way, isn't it strange . . . but it's true, no? And you must do something about that beard, will nothing make it grow . . . ? (*She laughs.*) What a funny boy you are!

Trofimov (*picks up the telegram*)   Why should I care if people don't find me attractive?

Lyubov Andreyevna   It's a telegram from Paris. I have a pile of them so high. One came yesterday, one today . . . The brute's ill again, in a dreadful state . . . Please, please will I forgive him, will I return . . . I ought to go, be with him for a while. Oh, what an angry face, but what else can I do, what must I do? He's sick, he's alone, he's unhappy, someone has to take care of him, stop him behaving like a fool, give him his medicine at the right time. Why am I forced to hide it? No, I won't bite my tongue, I love him, it's obvious anyway. I love, love . . . He's a lead weight round my neck, it'll drag me down to the bottom but I can't exist without him. (*She squeezes* **Trofimov**'s *hand.*) Don't criticise me, Petya, say nothing, don't speak at all . . .

Trofimov (*through tears*)   God forgive me but I have to say what I think: he stole everything you had!

Lyubov Andreyevna   No, no, you mustn't say that . . . (*She covers her ears.*)

Trofimov   He's a crook, you're the only one who can't see it. A cheap crook, that's all he is . . .

Lyubov Andreyevna (*irritated but controlling herself*)   How old are you? Twenty-six, twenty-seven, you carry on like a schoolboy!

Trofimov   And if I do?

Lyubov Andreyevna   Has no one taught you how grown-up men behave? Are you too young to know what love is? Find out, fall in love, why don't you? (*Angrily.*) I'm right! You go on and on about the purity of your soul, the fact is you're a prude, that's what, with a head full of infantile ideas, you're a joke . . . !

Trofimov (*horrified*)   Why are you saying this?

Lyubov Andreyevna   'Much more than a love affair!' You? No! As Firs would put it, 'You're useless!' Arrived at your great age and still hasn't got a lover!

Trofimov (*horrified*)   This is dreadful! Why's she saying this?

(*He hurries into the ballroom, clutching his head.*) Dreadful . . . I
can't, I'm going, I . . . (*He goes out and comes back at once.*)
Everything between us is over! (*He goes out into the entrance hall.*)

Lyubov Andreyevna (*shouting after him*)   Don't go! Petya!
Idiot, I was teasing you! Petya!

*Someone is heard running up the stairs in the entrance hall, then suddenly
falling downstairs with a crash.* **Anya** *and* **Varya** *cry out but at once
there comes the sound of laughter.*

Lyubov Andreyevna   What was that? What happened?

Anya *runs in.*

Anya (*laughing*)   Petya fell down the stairs! (*She runs out.*)

Lyubov Andreyevna   What a madman . . .

The **Station Master** *comes on, stands in the centre of the ballroom
and reads 'The Sinful Woman' by A. K. Tolstoy.*

Station Master

> 'The crowd moans, roars like a lion
> Decrying Rome whose hated yoke
> Bears down hard on the neck of the folk
> Whom Pilate rules with a rod of iron.
> But a tale's spread abroad of hope at hand.
> A mysterious stranger has appeared in the land . . .'

*People listen, but he has time to read only a few lines before the sound of a
waltz floats in from the entrance hall and the reading breaks off.*

Everyone dances. **Trofimov, Anya, Varya** *and* **Lyubov
Andreyevna** *come in from the entrance hall.*

Lyubov Andreyevna   Oh, Petya . . . you pure soul . . .
forgive me . . . dance with me. (*She dances with* **Trofimov**.)

Anya *and* **Varya** *dance.*

Firs *comes on and leans his stick against the side door.* **Yasha** *has
come in from the drawing room and is watching the dancing.*

Yasha   What's up with you, Grandpa?

Firs   I don't feel so good. In the old days, our guests were generals, barons, admirals, now we invite the post office clerk and the station master, and they think they're doing us a favour. Not good at all. In my day if someone got ill the late master, their grandfather, prescribed a teaspoon of sealing wax no matter what the complaint. I've taken a teaspoon of sealing wax every day for twenty years, which must be why I'm still alive.

Yasha   You're so boring, Grandpa. (*He yawns.*) Isn't it time you kicked the bucket?

Firs   Ach . . . ! You're useless! (*He mutters.*)

Trofimov *and* **Lyubov Andreyevna** *dance together, first in the ballroom then in the drawing room.*

Lyubov Andreyevna   *Merci*! I think I'll sit down for a while . . . (*She sits.*) I'm exhausted.

Anya *comes on.*

Anya (*agitated*)   In the kitchen someone's saying the cherry orchard's been sold.

Lyubov Andreyevna   Sold to whom?

Anya   He didn't say. And now he's gone.

She dances with **Trofimov**, *then they go into the ballroom.*

Yasha   It's some old fool spreading rumours. No one knows him, he's not from round here.

Firs   And Leonid Andreyevich's still not back. All he's wearing is his light overcoat, it's fine in the spring but . . . before you turn round he'll have caught a cold. Ach! Born yesterday . . .

Lyubov Andreyevna   I think I'm going to die. Yasha, find out who it was sold to.

Yasha   How can I? He disappeared ages ago. (*He laughs.*)

Lyubov Andreyevna (*slightly irritated*)   What are you laughing at? What's so amusing?

Yasha Yepikhodov, he's hilarious! Talks such rubbish. 'Just My Luck!'

Lyubov Andreyevna Firs, if the estate is sold, where will you go?

Firs Wherever you tell me to.

Lyubov Andreyevna What's the matter with your face? Are you ill? You ought to be in bed.

Firs Certainly . . . (*Smiling.*) I'll go to bed, then who'll serve the guests, who'll make sure everything's as it ought to be? There's only me in the whole house.

Yasha (*to* **Lyubov Andreyevna**) Madame, may I ask you a favour? If you go back to Paris, take me with you. I can't stay here, it's impossible. (*Looking round, speaking softly.*) What can I say about this place? Nothing you don't know, they're living in the Dark Ages, they have no idea of right and wrong. But the worst thing is it's so boring. The food they serve in the kitchen is unspeakable and I have to put up with Firs who doesn't know his place and spouts drivel. Let me go with you!

Pischik *comes on.*

Pischik May I have the honour? . . . one little waltz, you heavenly creature . . . (**Lyubov Andreyevna** *joins him.*) You've bewitched me, but even so I'll squeeze some money out of you . . . I will . . . (*They dance.*) One hundred and eighty . . . (*They go into the ballroom.*)

Yasha (*singing softly*)

'If you could see
my soul's misery . . .'

In the ballroom a figure in a grey top hat and check trousers can be seen waving its arms and leaping about. There are shouts of 'Bravo, Charlotta!'

Dunyasha (*she has stopped to powder her nose. To* **Firs**) Anya said: 'You must dance, there're so many men and not enough ladies,' I've danced so hard my head's spinning, my heart's pounding away, and then the post office clerk said something that almost made me scream.

The music gets softer.

Firs   What did he say?

Dunyasha   He said, 'You're as delicate as a flower.'

Yasha (*yawns*)   In the Dark Ages . . . (*He goes out.*)

Dunyasha   As delicate as a flower . . . I'm sensitive, when people say sweet things I melt.

Firs   You'll be in deep water before you know it.

Yepikhodov *comes on.*

Yepikhodov (*to* **Dunyasha**)   Been wondering where I am, I don't suppose? . . . treats me like a repellent little insect. (*He sighs.*) Ach! Life!

Dunyasha   What do you want now?

Yepikhodov   And quite possibly you're not incorrect! (*He sighs.*) However, to consider from a different vantage, it's you, excuse this blunt speech, who've produced in me this condition. My fate, each day something goes wrong, I withstand, which is to say the future I await with a smile. But you gave your word and even though I . . .

Dunyasha   We'll talk about it later, leave me, please. I feel as though I'm in a dream . . . (*She plays with her fan.*)

Yepikhodov   Each day some disaster, even so, smile, laugh . . .

Varya *comes in from the ballroom.*

Varya (*to* **Yepikhodov**)   Still hanging about? You've no respect for anything or anyone. Dunyasha, what are you doing here? Get out! (To **Yepikhodov**.) You play billiards, you break a cue, then parade up and down, do you imagine you're a guest in this house?

Yepikhodov   Pardon my saying, you've no call to interrogate my . . .

Varya Interrogating? I'm giving you an order. All day you saunter about, no work gets done. We employ you to keep the books, do you do it?

Yepikhodov (*offended*)   If I work or walk about or eat or play billiards, it's up to older and wiser than you to advance opinions.

Varya You dare take that tone with me? (*Flaring up.*) The nerve! So I'm a fool, is that it? Get out of here! This minute!

Yepikhodov (*cowed*)   Isn't it conceivable for you to address me in a manner more . . . ?

Varya (*exploding*)   Now! Out!

He goes towards the door. She follows him.

Varya 'Just My Luck!' If I catch even a glimpse of you in here . . . I never want to set eyes on you again!

Yepikhodov *goes out. His voice is heard: 'I'll file a complaint!'*

Varya Coming back for more, are you? (*She seizes the stick* **Firs** *left at the door.*) Come on . . . come on . . . I'll teach you . . . I'll give you something you're not expecting . . .

As she brandishes the stick, **Lopakhin** *comes on.*

Lopakhin Thank you very much.

Varya (*sneering angrily*)   Oh, frightfully sorry.

Lopakhin Not at all, I appreciate the warm welcome.

Varya Don't mention it. (*She moves away, then turns and speaks softly.*) I didn't hurt you?

Lopakhin It's nothing. Though there'll be rather a lump.

Voices in the ballroom: 'Lopakhin's here! Lopakhin's arrived!' **Pischik** *comes on.*

Pischik A sight for sore eyes! (*He exchanges kisses with* **Lopakhin**.) What's that I sniff? Brandy? Well, my friend, we too have been celebrating.

Lyubov Andreyevna *comes on.*

Lyubov Andreyevna (*to* **Lopakhin**)   You're here! What took so long? Where's my brother?

Lopakhin   We travelled back together, he'll be here any minute . . .

Lyubov Andreyevna (*agitated*)   Tell me! Did the auction take place? Say something!

Lopakhin (*confused, he tries to hide his joy*)   It was over by four . . . We missed the train so we had to wait for the next, at half past nine. (*He sighs heavily.*) Oof! My head's going round . . .

Gaev *comes on. In his right hand he holds various purchases, with his left he wipes away tears.*

Lyubov Andreyevna   Lyonya, what's wrong? Tell me, Lyonya! (*Impatient, in tears.*) Spit it out, for God's sake . . .

Gaev *dismisses her with a wave of his hand.*

Gaev (*to* **Firs**, *weeping*)   Take these . . . Anchovies, and herrings from Kerch . . . I've eaten nothing all day . . . So much has happened!

The door to the billiard room is open. The click of billiard balls can be heard and **Yasha** *saying: 'Seven and eighteen!'*

Gaev (*his expression changes, he stops crying*)   I'm worn out . . . Firs, help me change . . .

He goes to his room on the far side of the ballroom. **Firs** *follows.*

Pischik   What happened at the auction? Tell us!

Lyubov Andreyevna   Was the cherry orchard sold?

Lopakhin   It was.

Lyubov Andreyevna   Who bought it?

Lopakhin   I did.

It's as though a weight falls on **Lyubov Andreyevna**. *Only by holding on to an armchair and a table does she stop herself falling over.*

Varya *takes her bunch of keys from her belt, flings them on to the floor in the middle of the drawing room and goes out.*

Lopakhin   I bought the cherry orchard! Give me a moment, forgive me, everybody, my brain's whirling, I can't speak . . . (*He laughs.*) The auction. We arrived, Deriganov's already there. How much did your brother have to spend? Fifteen thousand? In his first bid Deriganov said he'd pay off the whole debt and offered thirty thousand on top. It's obvious which way the wind's blowing, so I took him on, I bid forty thousand. He forty-five. Me fifty-five. He went up by fives and I by tens . . . In the end I offer ninety thousand over and above the debt and it's knocked down to me. So it's mine! The orchard belongs to me! (*He laughs loudly.*) My God, can everyone hear what I'm saying? The cherry orchard belongs to me! Someone tell me I'm drunk, that I've gone mad, that the whole day has been a dream . . . (*He stamps his feet.*) But no one laugh at me! Oh, my father, my grandfather I wish you could climb out of your graves and see what's happened, little Yermolai, who you thrashed, who can hardly read, who had no shoes even in winter, has bought the finest estate in the world! The estate where my grandfather and my father were slaves, where they weren't allowed even into the kitchen! I'm asleep, I'm dreaming all this, none of it's happened . . . You long for something so you imagine it but you can't see it clearly, there's a thick mist . . . (*Smiling tenderly, he picks up the keys.*) She threw down the keys to make the point that she's not housekeeper here any longer. (*He jingles the keys.*) Well, that's how it is.

The orchestra tunes up.

Lopakhin   Musicians, play! I want to hear you! Everyone come and see Yermolai Lopakhin take an axe to the orchard, watch the trees come down! We'll build cottages and the lives of our grandchildren and great-grandchildren will be beautiful beyond anything we can imagine . . . Music! Begin!

The orchestra plays.

Lyubov Andreyevna *has sunk deep into a chair. She weeps bitterly.*

Lopakhin (*reproachfully*)   Explain to me, why didn't you listen to what I told you? Poor darling, you have such a good heart, but the orchard has gone and you won't get it back ever. (*In tears.*) Oh, I wish this was all over, everything we do turns out clumsy, disappointing, why is life like this, why?

Pischik (*takes* **Lopakhin** *under the arm and speaks quietly.*) She's crying. Let's go into the ballroom, leave her to get on with it . . . Let's go . . . (*He leads him into the ballroom.*)

Lopakhin   What's happening? Musicians, play louder! I can't hear you! From now on everything will be just how I want it! (*With irony.*) Here comes the new boss, the owner of the cherry orchard! (*He bumps into a small table and nearly knocks over a candelabra.*) It doesn't matter! I can pay for everything! (*He goes out with* **Pischik**.)

The ballroom and the drawing room are both empty except for **Lyubov Andreyevna**. *She sits huddled up, weeping bitterly.*

The music plays softly.

Anya *and* **Trofimov** *come on quickly.* **Anya** *goes to her mother and kneels.* **Trofimov** *stays at the entrance to the ballroom.*

Anya   Mother? . . . you're crying, why? You're so good, so kind, my sweet, my beautiful mother, I love you . . . I bless you. The cherry orchard's sold, it's gone for ever, accept it, don't cry. You have your whole life, Mother, and your pure, good soul . . . Come with me, come, we'll leave here, darling, let's go! . . . We'll plant a new orchard, far better than the old one. You'll see it and all at once everything will make sense to you, you'll feel joy, you will, joy like at the moment the sun goes down, and you'll smile, Mother! Let's go, my darling! Let's go . . .

Act Four

The same as Act One.

The curtains have gone from the windows and the paintings from the walls. Only a few pieces of furniture remain, stacked in a corner as though for sale. There's an overwhelming feeling of emptiness.

Near the door that leads outside and at the back of the stage suitcases, bundles and so on are piled up.

Lopakhin *stands and waits.* **Yasha** *holds a tray with glasses of champagne.*

In the entrance hall, **Yepikhodov** *ties a box together with rope.*

Through the open door on the left the voices of **Varya** *and* **Anya** *can be heard.*

From offstage at the back comes a murmur of other voices. It's the peasants who have come to say goodbye.

Gaev's voice   Thank you, my friends, I'm deeply grateful.

Yasha   People from all over the estate have come to say goodbye. In my opinion peasants have good hearts but their brains are rotten.

The murmur of voices fades away.

Lyubov Andreyevna *and* **Gaev** *come on from the entrance hall. She isn't crying but she's pale, her face trembles and she can't speak.*

Gaev   But Lyuba, to give them your purse! You have to stop doing that sort of thing! You have to!

Lyubov Andreyevna   What else could I do? What else could I do? (*They go out.*)

Lopakhin (*in the doorway, as they go*)   Before you leave, a glass of champagne. I didn't think to bring some from town, at the station they had only one bottle. (*Pause.*) What's the matter? You don't feel like it? (*He moves away from the door.*) If I'd known

I wouldn't have bothered. Fine, then I won't have any either.

Yasha *carefully puts the tray down on a chair.*

Lopakhin Have a glass, Yasha, might as well.

Yasha To those about to depart! And to those who'll remain, good luck to you! (*He drinks.*) This is champagne? No. Take my word for it.

Lopakhin But it cost me a fortune! (*Pause.*) It's freezing in here.

Yasha No one's bothered to light the stoves. Who cares? We're leaving. (*He laughs.*)

Lopakhin What's making you laugh?

Yasha I'm happy.

Lopakhin It's October but the sun's out, there's no wind, it could be summer. Perfect weather for building. (*Glancing at his watch, through the door.*) May I remind you: the train will leave in forty-six minutes! Which means in twenty minutes, no later, we must go to the station. So get a move on.

Trofimov *comes on from outside. He wears an overcoat.*

Trofimov Time to go. The horses have been brought round to the front. Where my galoshes are I've no idea. They've walked off. (*In the doorway.*) Anya, my galoshes, can't find them anywhere!

Lopakhin And I'm off to gloomy old Kharkov. I can take the same train. A whole winter in Kharkov. Since all of you arrived I've done nothing, idled about, not a single thought in my head. I hate not working. What do I do with my hands? If they're not busy they look peculiar, as though they don't belong to me.

Trofimov Soon we'll be gone, you can start being useful again.

Lopakhin Have a drink, go on.

Trofimov Not for me.

Lopakhin   So you're heading for Moscow?

Trofimov   Yes, I'll point them in the right direction, then tomorrow Moscow.

Lopakhin   I see . . . I'm sure the professors haven't started their lectures. They'll wait for you to arrive.

Trofimov   In what way does this . . . ?

Lopakhin   You've been at the university how many years now?

Trofimov   Oh think of something new. That joke's dead of old age and it was pretty dull to begin with. (*He searches for his galoshes.*) Listen, it's unlikely we'll meet again, so, as a parting gift, may I give you a word of advice? Don't wave your arms about! It's a bad habit, don't do it. And as for your plans for putting up cottages, your theory – in days to come the people who rent them will buy them and become full members of the community – it's just more arm waving . . . Even so, I feel some affection for you. You have delicate, sensitive fingers like an artist's and a delicate, sensitive soul . . .

Lopakhin (*embracing him*)   I'm fond of you too. Goodbye. Thank you for everything. Let me give you some money for the journey.

Trofimov   What for? I don't need it.

Lopakhin   But you have none at all!

Trofimov   I do. I finished a translation and got paid for it. Look, it's here in my pocket. But thanks all the same. (*Anxiously.*) But I can't find my galoshes!

Varya (*from another room*)   Take the dirty things! (*She throws a pair of rubber galoshes on to the stage.*)

Trofimov   Varya, why are you always so angry? Hm . . . These aren't mine!

Lopakhin   Last spring I planted fields and fields of poppies, I made a profit of forty thousand. When all the flowers were out, you'd never seen anything so beautiful. But my point is I made forty thousand, I can lend you as much money as you need. Why pull a face? Are my manners too crude for you? I'm a peasant . . . I say what I mean.

Trofimov   Your father was a peasant, mine sold medicines. What does that teach us about why we're such different human beings? Nothing.

Lopakhin *takes out his wallet.*

Trofimov   Put it away! . . . Offer me two hundred thousand, I still say no. I owe nobody anything, I'm free. There are two sorts of people obsessed with money: those who have too much and those who have none. None of that has any hold over me, it's dry leaves blowing in the wind. In my life, of what use are you? I observe you and walk on, confident, proud. Mankind is marching towards the greatest truth there is, towards the most profound joy, and in that march I'm way out in front.

Lopakhin   You think you'll get there?

Trofimov   I do. (*Pause.*) I'll get there or show others the way.

From far off, an axe can he heard striking a tree.

Lopakhin   Well, goodbye. Time to go. You and I pull faces at each other but life goes on, it's not bothered about us. You know, sometimes I work for hours without stopping, I don't get tired, and then ideas start to flow and the reason why I'm here on earth becomes absolutely clear to me. But would you believe how many people there are in Russia, my friend, who go on and on year after year with no sense of what it's all for? Well, so what? The earth doesn't stop spinning . . . I hear her brother's got a job at the bank, they'll pay him six thousand a year . . . He won't last, he's bone idle . . .

Anya (*in the doorway*)   Mother says don't cut down the cherry trees until we've gone.

Trofimov   I'd have thought you'd have a bit more feeling . . . (*He goes out through the entrance hall.*)

Lopakhin   I'll tell them . . . I do see what she . . . (*He goes out.*)

Anya   Has Firs gone to the hospital?

Yasha   I gave orders this morning. They'll have taken him by now.

Yepikhodov *crosses the room.*

Anya (*to* **Yepikhodov**)   Would you find out if Firs has been taken to the hospital?

Yasha (*offended*)   I told Yegor to do it this morning. You don't need to repeat yourself ten times.

Yepikhodov   The ancient Firs, I speak with authority, is not suited to repairs, he should join his ancestors. I envy him. (*He discovers he has put a suitcase on top of a hatbox, squashing it.*) There you are, naturally! Inevitably! (*He goes out.*)

Yasha (*mockingly*)   'Just My Luck' . . .

Varya (*in the doorway*)   Has Firs gone to the hospital?

Anya   Yes.

Varya   So why didn't they take my letter for the doctor?

Anya   We'll send it on . . . (*She goes out.*)

Varya (*from the next room*)   Where's Yasha? Tell him his mother's come to say goodbye to him.

Yasha (*waves his hand dismissively*)   I can't stand much more of this.

All this time **Dunyasha** *has been busy. Now* **Yasha** *is alone, she goes to him.*

Dunyasha   Can't you look at me for even a moment? You're going away . . . you're leaving me . . .

(*She weeps and throws herself on his neck.*)

Yasha   What are you blubbering about? (*He drinks champagne.*) In six days – Paris! Tomorrow we climb aboard the

express train, tring tring, gone! I can't believe it. *Vive la France!*
. . . I don't belong here, I can't breathe . . . everyone's so
ignorant . . . makes me sick. (*He drinks champagne.*) What are
you crying for? Be a good girl, then you'll have no reason to
cry.

Dunyasha (*powders herself looking in a little mirror*)   Will you
write to me from Paris? I was so in love with you, Yasha, so
deeply in love! You know how highly strung I am, Yasha!

Yasha   Here they come. (*He busies himself with the suitcases,
humming softly.*)

Lyubov Andreyevna, Gaev, Anya *and* **Charlotta** *come on.*

Gaev   Come, come, come. We're late already. (*Looking at*
Yasha.) Somebody stinks of herring!

Lyubov Andreyevna   Give me ten more minutes
then bring the carriages . . . (*She glances round the room.*)
Goodbye, my house, dear old grandpa house. When
winter's over and it's spring you'll be gone, they'll have
pulled you down. How much you've seen. (*She kisses* **Anya**
with deep feeling.) My own, my own, look how she glows, your
precious eyes sparkle like diamonds. You're happy? Very,
very happy?

Anya   Very, Mother! A new life is beginning!

Gaev (*cheerfully*)   So everything's all right now. Until the
moment the orchard was sold we were all so upset, we suffered
so deeply, but a decision was made, that was that, no way out,
and we all began to relax, a smile appeared here and there . . .
I've a position at the bank, I'm a financier . . . and down she
goes . . . and you, Lyuba, despite everything, look much
healthier.

Lyubov Andreyevna   Yes. My nerves are stronger, that's
true. (*She is handed her hat and overcoat.*) I sleep right through the
night. It's time. Yasha, my things. (*To* **Anya**.) Sweetheart,
we'll see each other soon . . . So off to Paris! I'll live on the
money your aunt sent us to buy the estate – bravo Yaroslavl! –
though how long it will last . . .

Anya You'll be back soon . . . won't you? I'll be waiting, I'll finish at school then I'll find work, I'll be able to help you. We'll read hundreds of books together . . . won't we, Mother? . . . (*She kisses her mother's hands.*) . . . and a wonderful new world will open in front of us . . . (*She thinks for a moment.*) Mother, you will come back?

Lyubov Andreyevna   I will, my darling, darling sweet . . . (*She embraces her.*)

Lopakhin *comes on.* **Charlotta** *hums softly.*

Gaev Charlotta's happy, she's singing!

Charlotta (*picks up a bundle that looks like a baby in a swaddling clothes*) Baby, baby, bye bye, baby . . . (*The baby's cry is heard: Wah! Wah!*) Be quiet, my darling, my little boy. (*Wah! Wah!*) I'm so full of sorrow for you! (*She throws the bundle back where it was.*) So who will give me a new position? To stay here now is impossible.

Lopakhin We'll find you something, don't worry.

Gaev Everyone's deserting us. Varya's leaving . . . all at once we're of no use to anyone.

Charlotta I must move to town but I have nowhere to live . . . (*She hums.*) So what? It's all the same . . .

Pischik *comes on.*

Lopakhin Now look what the cat's dragged in!

Pischik (*out of breath*) Oof, let me catch my breath . . . I'm worn out . . . dear friends . . . water, water . . .

Gaev After money, I suppose? I shall remove myself from danger . . . (*He goes out.*)

Pischik It's ages since I was here . . . gorgeous creature . . . (*To* **Lopakhin**.) You here too? . . . glad to see you . . . most intelligent man I ever came across . . . here . . . for you . . . (*He gives* **Lopakhin** *money*.) . . . that's four hundred . . . which leaves eight hundred and forty I owe you . . .

Lopakhin (*astonished, shrugging his shoulders*)   Wake me up! . . . where did you get it from?

Pischik   In a minute . . . I'm boiling over . . . extraordinary event occurred. Some Englishmen appeared at my house, dug up some white clay . . . (*To* **Lyubov Andreyevna**.) And four hundred for you . . . you bewitching, glorious . . . (*He gives her money.*) You'll get the rest in a few days. (*He drinks water.*) In the train, I heard a young man quoting some marvellous philosopher. His advice to the world is: 'Climb on to the roof, then jump off . . . Jump!' – he says, that's it! (*Astonished.*) Extraordinary! Water, water . . .

Lopakhin   What Englishmen are these?

Pischik   I sold them a lease on the land with the white clay for twenty-four years . . . However, forgive me, in a rush . . . must run along . . . off to Znoikov's . . . and Kardamonov's . . . I owe everyone money! (*He drinks.*) Good health to you all . . . I'll drop by on Thursday . . .

Lyubov Andreyevna   We're about to go into town, tomorrow I'm leaving Russia . . .

Pischik   You're what? (*Alarmed.*) Into town? What for? Oh. Furniture . . . suitcases . . . well, never mind . . . (*Through tears.*) Never mind . . . most extraordinary people I've ever met, those English . . . never mind . . . be happy . . . May God look after you . . . it doesn't matter . . . everything in the world comes to an end . . . (*He kisses* **Lyubov Andreyevna**'s *hand.*) And if one day someone tells you my end has come, think of this old horse and say: 'Once upon a time there was a certain man . . . Simeonov-Pischik . . . may he rest in peace' . . . weather's looking up . . . extraordinary . . . (*He goes out very distressed, then comes back and speaks from the doorway.*) My Dashenka sends her best wishes! (*He goes.*)

Lyubov Andreyevna   Now we can go. I'm leaving with two stones on my heart. The first is Firs, he's ill. (*She glances at her watch.*) We can stay, I think, five more minutes . . .

Anya   Mother, Firs is at the hospital. Yasha sent him this morning.

Lyubov Andreyevna   The other is Varya. Her life's been getting up at dawn, working right through the day. Now what will she do with herself? Have you noticed how thin she's become, and pale? And she's in tears all the time, poor thing . . . (*Pause. To* **Lopakhin**.) You know perfectly well my dream was that you and she would marry, there were times it seemed quite likely. (*She whispers to* **Anya** *who nods to* **Charlotta**. *They both go out.*) She adores you, you've shown signs of tenderness towards her, I don't know, I don't know, I think the two of you deliberately avoid each other. It's ridiculous!

Lopakhin   I'll be honest with you, I don't understand it either. Everything about it's so strange . . . Is it too late? If not I'm prepared to . . . even right now, what do you think? . . . Why don't we do it and it's done. Once you've gone I'll never get round to it.

Lyubov Andreyevna   Wonderful! How long can it take? Half a minute, that's all. I'll call her . . .

Lopakhin   As it happens there's champagne. (*He looks at the glasses.*) Empty, someone's polished it off.

Yasha *coughs.*

Lopakhin   Drunk it all, dirty dog . . .

Lyubov Andreyevna (*excitedly*)   This is perfect! I'll leave you to it . . . Yasha, *allez!* I'll call her . . . (*In the doorway.*) Varya, put everything down and come here. Hurry up! (*She goes out with* **Yasha**.)

Lopakhin (*glances at his watch*)   So . . .

Pause.

From behind the door comes suppressed laughter, then whispering, then at last **Varya** *comes on.*

Varya (*examines everything for a long time*)   Odd, I've looked everywhere for . . .

Lopakhin   What've you lost?

Varya   I packed it myself, but can I find it?

Pause.

Lopakhin   Where will you go?

Varya   Me? To the Ragulins . . . I've said I'll look after things for them . . . be their housekeeper, more or less.

Lopakhin   They're at Yashnevo, am I right? Not that far away. (*Pause.*) So, for this house it's over . . .

Varya   Where is it? . . . Or did I put it in the trunk? . . . Yes, for this house, that's it . . . no more, never . . .

Lopakhin   I'm off to Kharkov . . . taking the same train as . . . Lots to do. I'm leaving Yepikhodov in charge here . . . I've taken him on.

Varya   You what?

Lopakhin   This time last year – do you remember? – there was snow on the ground, today the sun's out, there's no wind. Though there is a nip in the air . . . and this morning there was frost.

Varya   Was there? I didn't notice . . . (*Pause.*) Besides which, our thermometer's broken . . .

Pause.

From outside, a voice calls: 'Lopakhin!'

Lopakhin (*as though he's been waiting for this*)   Coming! (*He goes out quickly.*)

Varya *sits on the floor, lays her head on a bundle of clothes and weeps softly. The door opens,* **Lyubov Andreyevna** *comes in warily.*

Lyubov Andreyevna   And? (*Pause.*) Time to go.

Varya (*she has already stopped crying. She wipes her eyes*)   Yes, it's time. I won't get to the Ragulins today if you miss your train . . .

Lyubov Andreyevna (*in the doorway*)   Anya, get ready!

Anya *comes on, then* **Gaev** *and* **Charlotta**. **Gaev** *wears a warm overcoat with a hood. Servants and Drivers gather.* **Yepikhodov** *fusses with everything.*

Lyubov Andreyevna At last we're on our way.

Anya (*joyfully*) We're on our way!

Gaev My friends, dear, kind friends! As we depart from this house for the last time, I feel it incumbent to express the deep emotion that suffuses every inch of my . . .

Anya (*imploringly*) Uncle!

Varya Uncle, don't!

Gaev (*cast down*) The yellow into the corner pocket . . . My lips are sealed . . .

Trofimov *comes on, then* **Lopakhin**.

Trofimov Come on, everyone, time to go!

Lopakhin Yepikhodov, my coat!

Lyubov Andreyevna I want to sit for one tiny moment more. These walls, I feel I've never seen them, never taken them in, or the ceiling, I feel I could stare at them for ever, they seem so precious to me . . .

Gaev It comes back to me, I was six years old, Trinity Sunday, I sat at this window and watched my father setting off to church . . .

Lyubov Andreyevna Have we got everything?

Lopakhin I think so. (*To* **Yepikhodov**, *putting on his overcoat.*) I want you to follow my instructions to the letter.

Yepikhodov (*hoarse*) Don't worry, I will.

Lopakhin What's wrong with your voice?

Yepikhodov I drank some water, went down the wrong way.

Yasha (*with contempt*) Barbarians . . . !

Lyubov Andreyevna   We'll be gone – and not a soul will be here . . .

Lopakhin   Until the spring.

Varya *pulls an umbrella out of a bundle, as though brandishing it.*
Lopakhin *makes a face as though he were afraid.*

Varya   What . . .? Did you think . . .? No, I didn't mean to . . .

Trofimov   Everyone, into the carriages . . . we must go! The train's about to arrive!

Varya   Petya, they're here, your galoshes, by this suitcase. (*In tears.*) They're so dirty, so worn out . . .

Trofimov (*putting on his galoshes*)   Everyone, let's go!

Gaev (*very upset, afraid of bursting into tears*)   Train . . . railway station . . . sink the blue, white off the middle cushion . . .

Lyubov Andreyevna   Let's go!

Lopakhin   Is everyone here? We haven't left anyone behind? (*He locks the door on the left.*) I've put everything of value in there, it must be kept locked. Let's go!

Anya   Goodbye, house! Goodbye, old life!

Trofimov   Welcome, new life! (*He goes out with* **Anya**.)

Varya *looks round the room, then goes out in her own time.* **Yasha** and **Charlotta**, *holding her dog, go out.*

Lopakhin   That's it till spring. Off we go, everybody . . . Farewell! (*He goes out.*)

Lyubov Andreyevna *and* **Gaev** *have been waiting for the moment when they are alone together. They throw themselves on each other's necks, sobbing gently so they won't be overheard.*

Gaev (*in despair*)   My sister, my sister . . .

Lyubov Andreyevna   Oh, my beautiful orchard! . . . My life, my childhood, my happiness, goodbye! . . . Goodbye! . . .

Anya's voice (*calling cheerfully*)   Mother!

Trofimov's voice (*cheerful, excited*)   Where are you . . .?

Lyubov Andreyevna   One last look . . . the walls, the windows . . . Mother loved to stroll round this room . . .

Gaev   My sister, my sister . . . !

Anya's voice   Mother . . . !

Trofimov's voice   Where are you . . .?

Lyubov Andreyevna   We're coming! (*They go out.*)

The stage is empty.

The sound of a key locking all the doors, then the carriages are heard driving away. It grows quiet.

Amid the silence, the dull thud of an axe against a tree rings out, desolate and sad.

Steps are heard. Through the door on the right, **Firs** *comes on, dressed, as always, in a jacket, a white waistcoat and slippers. He is ill.*

Firs (*goes to the door and tries the handle*)   Locked. They've gone . . . (*He sits on the divan.*) And me? They forgot . . . Never mind . . . I'll sit here a minute . . . I'll bet Leonid Andreyevich isn't wearing his fur coat, he'll have put on the cotton one . . . (*He sighs anxiously.*) I didn't have a chance to check . . . What do they know? Born yesterday . . . (*He mumbles inaudibly.*) Life begins, ends, when do you find time to live it . . . ? (*He lies down.*) I'll lie here a minute . . . No strength, none left, not a drop . . . Ach, you're useless. (*He lies still.*)

From far away, a sound rings out. It's as though there came from the sky the sound of a string breaking, then dying away mournfully.

Silence.

Then the only thing that can be heard is an axe, far away in the orchard, thudding against a tree.

Printed in the United States
148609LV00001B/5/A

9 780413 757807